M^cCALL'S PRESENTS
THE
WORKING MOTHER
COOKBOOK

M^cCALL'S PRESENTS
THE
WORKING MOTHER
COOKBOOK

BY THE EDITORS OF *WORKING MOTHER* MAGAZINE
with Herbert T. Leavy

Macmillan Publishing Company
New York

**This Book was prepared by
Books from Magazines, Inc.,
Herbert T. Leavy, president**

Macmillan Publishing Company
866 Third Avenue, New York, N.Y. 10022
Collier Macmillan Canada, Inc.

Library of Congress Cataloging in Publication Data
Main entry under title:
McCall's presents the Working mother cookbook.
   1. Cookery. I. Leavy, Herbert T. II. Working mother
(New York, N.Y.: 1981) III. Title: Working mother
cookbook.
TX652.M36 1985   641.5   84-25103
ISBN 0-02-631560-2

Macmillan books are available at special discounts
for bulk purchases for sales promotions, premiums,
fund-raising, or educational use. Special editions
or book excerpts can also be created to specifica-
tion. For details, contact:

Special Sales Director
Macmillan Publishing Company
866 Third Avenue
New York, New York 10022

10 9 8 7 6 5 4 3 2 1

Printed in the United States of America

Acknowledgments

Herbert T. Leavy of *Books from Magazines, Inc.*, is indebted to the following people for their gracious help in the production of this book, which is totally based on the editorial resources of *Working Mother* magazine: Richard M. King, vice president and director of McCall's Enterprises; Vivian Cadden, editor of *Working Mother* magazine, Mary McLaughlin, managing editor, Katherine Minton, food editor; Melinda Corey of Macmillan Publishing Company; Janet Schuy for her expert typing and proofreading skills; Mary Shanahan Kuefner for her culinary advice; and the following food writers: Patricia Cobe, Judy Gorman, Joanne Hayes, Karen MacNeil, Karen Pritzker, Joanna Pruess, Cynthia Sternau, and Yvonne Young Tarr.

Contents

McCALL'S PRESENTS
THE
WORKING MOTHER
COOKBOOK

INTRODUCTION:
WHAT THIS BOOK
IS ALL ABOUT

Besides death and taxes, one other thing is inevitable: The family must eat. This means, of course, the family must be fed—usually by you—day in and day out, on weekdays and weekends, in fair weather and foul.

Do you recognize this scene? It's 7:00 A.M. Nathaniel can't find his report on *The Cricket in Times Square*, and it's due today. Jenny is stalling in her room. She doesn't want to wear that yukky skirt, but all her jeans are in the laundry basket. Your husband is explaining that he can't get the car to the mechanic's and that you'll have to drop it off on your way to work and take the bus the last ten blocks. Meanwhile, you are contemplating the nearly empty milk carton and wondering what to fix for breakfast now that cereal is not possible.

Or perhaps this scenario is closer to the mark: You've had an absolutely rotten day at the office. The printer didn't deliver the price sheets he had promised, and the salespeople had to take outdated ones on their calls. The boss was furious at you, not the printer. Then you got stuck in traffic and had to wait 20 minutes for a tow truck to remove an overturned trailer from your freeway exit. You've just come in the door, and two chatterboxes are vying to give you the bulletins from school. Your husband is seated before the television set watching the evening news. When the commercial comes on, he acknowledges your presence with a cheery, "What's for dinner?"

You do not feel like answering the question. In fact, you don't feel like making dinner. (This is surely the understatement of the year.) However, the only other option seems to be to go back out the door, jump in the car, and see what's doing on the freeway.

So, of course, you'll go into the kitchen and make dinner. (Spaghetti, perhaps, since you forgot to take a chicken out of the freezer this morning.) After all, there must be some reward for all the aggravation you've had today, and what else could be better than sitting down to a good meal with the people you love? What are you knocking yourself out for anyway? Isn't good food shared with your family one of life's great pleasures?

Well, perhaps you aren't in the frame of mind to see it this way just now because having the job of cook—when you already have a full-time job—is very hard indeed. It's plain to see *you need some help.*

That's where this book comes in. It shows you ways to get food on the table as painlessly as possible. Good food. Even great food. There are sections on most of the problems working mothers must solve. There's one, for instance, on avoiding the scene just described. It's the chapter called "You Start the Dinner, and I'll Finish When I Get Home." It's full of easy recipes that a child or a babysitter or a husband could begin. There are even safety rules for young or inexperienced chefs. But the best thing of all is that each recipe leaves very little for you to do. The upshot is that your starving family can sit down to a delicious meal about a half hour after you—the master chef—get home!

Then there's a chapter that addresses the dinner problem in another way. It's called "Relax While It Cooks." The idea here is that you quickly assemble a few ingredients, put them on top of the stove or into the oven to cook for 45 minutes, then you go and put your feet up in the living room and relax with your husband while the whole family spills out the news of the day.

Of course, there's more to feeding the family than serving supper. There's the daily question of what to fix for breakfast and what to put in the kids' lunchboxes, and maybe into your own and your husband's as well. To these questions there are plenty of answers. None of them are difficult and none need careful study. After all, there's nothing wrong with some coffee or juice and a bowl of cereal and milk in the morning—even every day—as long as everyone will eat it. What you need are suggestions for those times when you'd like a little change. This philosophy holds for lunchbox fare as well. If the children are content with a peanut butter sandwich and an apple, be grateful and let them make the sandwich themselves. (We don't need to point out that the more you can get them to do, the happier you—and they—will be!)

Which brings us to that time of day when kids come home and head straight for the refrigerator. We've got lots of suggestions for snacks they can make themselves. If they are old enough to scrape a carrot, spread a graham cracker with cottage cheese, and pour themselves a glass of milk, they're old enough to snack on their own. Just give them this book when they run out of ideas.

All these ideas, by the way, require something we haven't mentioned: food in the refrigerator and staples in the cupboard. Stocking the larder so that your family members can feed themselves when need be is another task that must be faced once or twice a week—unless you are a really super organizer and can shop for two weeks without forgetting one single thing! But our advice on stocking up is to get someone else to do it. Your husband seems an extremely likely candidate. (See Appendix II—"Supermarket Strategy" for more on this.)

And that brings up the major point of the book. If you are going to take full responsibility for all the meals the family eats, this book will certainly help you. But it could be useful to you in quite another way. We hope you'll share it so that *everyone* will help. Eating is a family affair, and it's nice when everyone pitches in. Even a two-year-old can begin to take part in the ritual and to learn that producing a meal is everyone's work. He or she will get the idea by being responsible for putting a napkin in each place or for taking his (her) plate to the sink when dinner is done. And your husband can be your biggest ally in the food department. He can share the fun of experimenting with recipes you'll be trying and enjoying. This is a *family* cookbook!

MARY MCLAUGHLIN
Managing Editor

CHAPTER ONE

RELAX WHILE
IT COOKS

The idea of this chapter is to give you a breather—a time to be with your family, play with the baby, read a bedtime story to the toddler, let the schoolchildren pour out their news, and maybe even relax with your husband. The meals can go unwatched on top of the stove or in the oven while you have a chance to unwind. Dessert for these weekday dinners, unless you've fixed it on the weekend, can be fruit and cheese or ice cream, cookies, or cake on hand.

1. Start these dinners in 15 minutes or less.
2. Forget them for 45 minutes.
3. Get them on the table in 15 minutes or less.

BEEF MENUS AND RECIPES

SWISS STEAK
POPPY-SEED NOODLES
GREEN BEANS

SWISS STEAK

- 4 tablespoons flour
- 1 tablespoon dry mustard
- 3–4 cube steaks
- 1 large onion, thinly sliced
- 1 cup sliced mushrooms
- 2 beef bouillon cubes
- 1 tablespoon Worcestershire sauce
- 1 cup sour cream

In a bowl, combine flour and mustard. Sprinkle some of flour mixture over each steak. Rub in well; repeat on the other side. Set aside remaining flour mixture.

Coat bottom of a skillet with oil. Brown steaks over medium-high heat. Arrange onion slices and mushrooms over steaks. Add ½ cup of water, bouillon cubes, and Worcestershire, and bring to a boil. Reduce heat to low, and cover.

Fixing time: about 10 minutes.

Relax for 45 minutes.

Return to the kitchen. Uncover skillet and stir onions and mushrooms into liquid in skillet. Simmer, uncovered, for 10 minutes. Bring a pot of salted water to a boil. Drop noodles into boiling water and then prepare frozen green beans.

Remove skillet from heat. Transfer steaks to a platter. Stir remaining flour mixture into sour cream and stir into liquid in skillet. Cook several minutes over medium heat, stirring, until it thickens; do not boil. Spoon sauce over steaks.

Drain noodles in a colander and transfer to a serving dish. Toss with butter and sprinkle on some poppy seeds. Drain beans and place in a serving dish with a little butter.

Time from kitchen to table: 15 minutes.

Serves 3–4.

BEEF SHORT RIBS WITH YOGURT SAUCE
RICE PILAF
CHERRY TOMATOES AND CELERY STICKS
CRUSTY BREAD

BEEF SHORT RIBS WITH YOGURT SAUCE

Oil
4 lbs beef short ribs, cut into serving pieces
1 cup beef broth
1 large onion, chopped
1 clove garlic, minced
2 teaspoons thyme
1 teaspoon basil
1 tablespoon cornstarch
1 cup plain yogurt

Preheat oven to 375° F.

Pour enough oil into a Dutch oven to just cover bottom. Add ribs, place over medium-high heat, and cook until well browned. Pour off fat.

Add beef broth to pan and bring to a boil. Turn off heat. Sprinkle onion, garlic, thyme, and basil over ribs. Cover pan and place in oven.

Fixing time: 15 minutes.

Relax for 45 minutes.

Return to the kitchen. Uncover Dutch oven and turn ribs over with a pair of tongs. Let meat continue to cook, uncovered, while you prepare rice pilaf and vegetables. Wash tomatoes and celery, and prepare 4 servings of packaged rice pilaf.

Remove pan from oven and transfer ribs to a platter. Skim fat from pan juices. Dissolve cornstarch in 2 tablespoons of water and add to pan. Stir over high heat until thickened. Reduce heat to medium and blend in yogurt. Warm through but do not boil. Spoon sauce over ribs.

Transfer rice to a serving dish. You're ready to eat.

Time from kitchen to table: 10 minutes.

Serves 4.

OLD-FASHIONED POT ROAST
POTATOES IN THEIR JACKETS
BUTTERED BROCCOLI
WARM BISCUITS
HOT CIDER WITH CINNAMON

OLD-FASHIONED POT ROAST

  1 tablespoon butter
    One 3-lb beef roast (top or bottom round)
  2 medium onions
  ½ teaspoon salt
    Dash of pepper
  ¼ teaspoon thyme
  ¼ cup coffee
  2 tablespoons catsup
  2 tablespoons flour

Heat butter in a 6-quart pressure cooker. Dry meat with paper towels and sauté in butter until browned on all sides.

Slice onions. Place them around and on top of roast. Sprinkle with salt, pepper, and thyme. Pour 1½ cups of water around roast. Mix together coffee and catsup; pour over meat mixture.

Cover pan and set control at 10 pounds of pressure. Place over high heat until control jiggles. Reduce heat and cook for 45 minutes, following manufacturer's directions for 10 pounds of pressure.

Scrub 4–6 baking potatoes and place in a large saucepan. Add water to cover and bring to a boil. Reduce heat and simmer for 45 minutes.

Fixing time: 15 minutes.

Relax for 45 minutes.

Return to the kitchen. Turn off heat under roast. Let cool 5 minutes. Prepare frozen broccoli according to package directions and warm some prepared biscuits.

Drain potatoes well; keep warm or put in toaster oven to crisp skins.

Place pressure cooker under cold running water to reduce pressure. Remove roast to serving platter, reserving pan juices. Combine flour with ⅓ cup of water. Skim fat from juices in pan. Stir in flour mixture and cook until thickened. Pour into bowl or gravy boat.

Time from kitchen to table: 15 minutes.

Serves 4–6.

Tip:

Save single portions of leftovers by freezing as a "TV dinner" in a foil tray or pie plate. If you do this several times, you will have a collection on hand for a night when you have to make dinner in a hurry, and your family will enjoy having some choices.

CHILI CON CARNE
RICE
GARNISH OF SOUR CREAM AND ONIONS
TOSSED GREEN SALAD
ICE-COLD BEER OR ICE-COLD MILK

CHILI CON CARNE

- 1½ lbs chopped chuck
- 2–4 cloves garlic, diced
- 1 big sweet onion, finely chopped
- 2 cans (20-oz size) red kidney beans
  - Chili powder
  - Garlic powder (optional)
  - Salt and pepper
- 1 pt sour cream

Put a big skillet on top of stove over medium heat and let pan warm up. Crumble meat into skillet and brown gently, using a fork to break up meat. Add garlic and about three-fourths of chopped onion.

While meat mixture simmers, put kidney beans in a large saucepan over low heat. Add meat mixture and 2–3 tablespoons of chili powder, 1–2 vigorous shakes of garlic powder, and salt and pepper to taste. Cover pan.

Prepare rice according to directions on package. After you have added rice to boiling water, cover and turn down heat to lowest setting.

Fixing time: about 10 minutes.

Relax for 30 minutes.

Return to the kitchen. Check rice. Taste chili and add more chili powder and other seasonings if necessary. Skim off any fat that may have collected. Put sour cream and chopped onions in serving bowls. Make a simple green salad and add prepared dressing. Bring everything to table and serve rice and chili in soup plates.

Serve piping hot, garnished with cold sour cream and a sprinkling of chopped sweet onion. (The warmed-up leftovers are great as a filling for pita bread or tacos—with the addition of sour cream and onions or chopped green peppers and shredded iceberg lettuce.)

Time from kitchen to table: about 10 minutes.

Serves 4–6.

PEPPER STEAK DINNER
BOSTON LETTUCE AND BROCCOLI SALAD
WARM FRENCH BREAD
CANNED PURPLE PLUMS

PEPPER STEAK DINNER

　　Oil for browning
1　lb boneless chuck (¾ inch thick)
　　Flour for dredging
1　large onion
1　large green pepper
½　teaspoon salt
1　can (16-oz size) stewed tomatoes
4　(about 1¼ lbs) baking potatoes

Preheat oven to 375° F.

Put some oil in a 3-quart Dutch oven; place over high heat to warm. Cut chuck into strips 1½ inches wide and dredge in some flour. Add meat to Dutch oven and sauté until well browned. Peel and slice onion. Wash and slice green pepper. Add both to Dutch oven. Sprinkle with salt. Pour tomatoes over all. Cover pan and place in oven. Scrub potatoes, pierce with a fork or knife, and put in oven.

Fixing time: 10 minutes.

Relax for 45 minutes.

Return to the kitchen. Remove pan from oven. If meat is tender, and potatoes are done, turn off oven. If not, return pan to oven and cook until done. Prepare salad and warm bread.

BOSTON LETTUCE AND BROCCOLI SALAD

1　head Boston lettuce
½　bunch broccoli
½　cup prepared oil and vinegar salad dressing

Separate, wash, and drain lettuce. Wash and drain broccoli. Break lettuce into a serving bowl. Trim off tough parts of broccoli stems. Slice broccoli lengthwise through florets, as thinly as possible. Add to lettuce. To serve, toss with dressing.

Time from kitchen to table: 15 minutes.

Serves 4.

CHINESE PEPPER STEAK
RICE
ROMAINE, ORANGE, AND WALNUT SALAD

CHINESE PEPPER STEAK

1½ lbs round steak (½ inch thick), cut into strips
  2 tablespoons oil
1½ cups water
  4 tablespoons soy sauce
  ¼ teaspoon garlic powder
  2 cups diced celery
  1 cup halved fresh mushrooms
  1 can (8-oz size) water chestnuts, drained and sliced
  1 green pepper, seeded and cut into strips
  2 tablespoons cornstarch dissolved in ¼ cup cold water

In a large, heavy saucepan over moderately high heat, brown meat on all sides in oil. Add water, soy sauce, and garlic powder, and stir well. Cover pan and reduce heat to moderately low.

Fixing time: under 10 minutes.

Relax for 45 minutes.

Return to the kitchen. Add celery, mushrooms, water chestnuts, and green pepper to meat mixture; stir to combine. Cover and continue cooking over low heat.

Prepare rice according to package directions.

Wash and dry romaine lettuce. Tear into pieces and put in a large salad bowl. Peel a navel orange, separate into sections, and add to bowl. Add ¼ cup of walnut halves. Toss salad with Italian dressing.

Remove cover from meat. Add cornstarch and water mixture; cook and stir until liquid thickens. Turn off heat. Serve meat and vegetables over rice.

Time from kitchen to table: 15 minutes.

Serves 4.

BAKED VEAL WITH YOGURT SAUCE
NOODLES
BUTTERED PEAS

BAKED VEAL WITH YOGURT SAUCE

   1 lb veal cubes for stewing
   2 tablespoons flour
     Oil
1½ teaspoons paprika
   2 cups plain yogurt
   1 cup sliced mushrooms
     Juice of ½ lemon
   2 tablespoons chopped parsley
     Salt and pepper to taste
     Parsley sprigs for garnish

Preheat oven to 350° F.

Dredge veal cubes in flour and shake off excess. Pour enough oil into a Dutch oven to just cover bottom. Add veal cubes and cook, stirring, over high heat until meat is browned.

Remove pan from heat. Sprinkle paprika over veal. Add yogurt, mushrooms, lemon juice, parsley, salt, and pepper. Return pan to heat; stir over medium heat until bubbling. Cover and place in oven.

Fixing time: 15 minutes.

Relax for 45 minutes.

Return to the kitchen. Stir veal mixture gently and let it continue to cook. Put a large pot of salted water on to boil for the noodles. When water comes to a boil, drop in noodles.

Prepare peas according to package directions.

Drain noodles in a colander and mound them in the center of a serving platter. Spoon veal and sauce around noodles; garnish with parsley sprigs. Drain peas and place in a serving dish with a pat of butter. Bring everything to table. You're ready to eat.

Time from kitchen to table: 15 minutes.

Serves 3–4.

SMOTHERED VEAL CHOPS
BAKED POTATOES
WATERCRESS AND ENDIVE SALAD
ICE TEA OR CHILLED WHITE WINE
OR MILK

SMOTHERED VEAL CHOPS

- 1 egg
- ½ cup seasoned bread crumbs
- 1 scant tablespoon vegetable oil
- 2 large shoulder veal chops
- 1 sweet onion, thinly sliced
- 1 green pepper, cored and sliced
- 1 jar (15½-oz size) prepared marinara spaghetti sauce

Preheat oven to 375° F.

Break egg into a shallow bowl and beat well with 2 tablespoons of water. Pour seasoned bread crumbs onto a plate. Heat vegetable oil in a Dutch oven on top of stove. Dip chops into egg, then into bread crumbs. Put chops into Dutch oven and brown lightly on both sides. Remove pot from heat.

Arrange sliced onion and pepper over chops and cover everything with marinara sauce. Raise chops with a fork so a little sauce covers bottom of pot. Put a lid on Dutch oven and put into oven.

Scrub 4 small baking potatoes, pierce each with a knife in several places, and place on oven rack.

Fixing time: 15 minutes.

Relax for 45 minutes.

Return to the kitchen. Fix the salad.

WATERCRESS AND ENDIVE SALAD

- 1 bunch watercress
- 2 heads endive
- ½ cup bottled Italian dressing

Rinse watercress and endive, and dry thoroughly. Pull leaves from endive and put in a salad bowl. Break watercress leaves in half and add to bowl. Toss greens with dressing.

Remove casserole from oven and test chops for doneness; a fork should pierce meat easily. Cut each chop in half. Now test potatoes the same way. If meat and potatoes are done, bring them and salad to table. You're ready to eat.

Time from kitchen to table: 10 minutes.

Serves 4.

MEATLOAF	MEATLOAF
TOMATO SAUCE	MUSHROOM GRAVY
BAKED POTATOES	NOODLES, RICE, OR
CAULIFLOWER OR	STUFFING
BUTTERED CARROTS	FRENCH-CUT BEANS, PEAS,
OR TOSSED SALAD	OR MIXED VEGETABLES
	OR TOSSED SALAD

TWO-DAY MEATLOAF

  2 lbs ground beef, or 1½ lbs ground beef and
    ½ lb ground lean pork
  ½ cup flavored bread crumbs
  2 eggs
  1 medium onion, chopped
  1 tablespoon Worcestershire sauce
1½ teaspoons salt
    Freshly ground pepper

Put all ingredients into a bowl and mix with your hands just long enough to combine everything. Line a baking dish with aluminum foil, using a piece big enough to hang over the edges. Place meat mixture on lined pan and shape into a loaf or, if you wish, into two loaves. Two squat loaves will bake more quickly than one high one. Shape loaf loosely so that end result has a nice consistency. Scrub and pierce a baking potato for each person. Put meatloaf and potatoes in a 350° F oven.

Fixing time: under 10 minutes.

Forget it for an hour.

Return to the kitchen. Take meatloaf out of oven. Test potatoes, and if by any chance they are not done, turn oven up to 450° F for 5 minutes. Heat a cup of prepared tomato sauce and start vegetable. Remove half of meatloaf you won't be using and set aside. Skim off fat around remaining meatloaf in pan and pour hot tomato sauce around loaf to mix with drippings. Serve meatloaf sliced on a platter with some sauce spooned over it and with more sauce in a gravy boat.

If you are serving remainder of meatloaf the next day, store it whole in refrigerator. If you are freezing it for another time, slice and wrap each piece separately in aluminum foil for easy thawing or just in case you want to use only part of it.

Time from kitchen to table: 10 minutes.

The second time around, you're in clover—whether you use meatloaf the next day or have frozen it. Put meatloaf slices in a skillet, surround with mushroom gravy made from canned or dehydrated mushroom soup, and doctor as you please with some wine or sherry. Cover skillet and heat through slowly. Fix noodles, rice, or stuffing, and a vegetable.

Time from kitchen to table: 10 minutes.

Serves 4 people generously at 2 meals.

This basic meatloaf recipe can be varied in many ways as you become familiar with it. Before the price of veal went out of sight, the combination of chopped meats could have been 1 pound of beef, ½ pound of veal, and ½ pound of pork or, for an especially delicious loaf, 1½ pounds of veal and ½ pound of pork.

Instead of seasoned bread crumbs, you can use plain crumbs or three slices of bread moistened with ½ cup of milk and do your own seasoning. Fresh chopped parsley, a dash of tabasco, or 2 tablespoons of prepared mustard are some of the possible additions.

With another ½ cup of crumbs, bringing the total to 1 full cup, you can make this already thrifty dish stretch even further. In that case, however, you will need to add another egg or ½ cup of catsup to keep the mixture moist enough.

If you have chopped onions on hand for this recipe, you can cut the preparation time almost in half. In fact, the existence of chopped onions, whether frozen or previously done in a food processor and stored in the refrigerator, is probably the greatest boon to the weekday cook. (There are some people who feel the same way about a ready supply of sliced onions.)

If you wish to substitute for the chopped onion and salt a dehydrated onion soup or a combination dehydrated onion and mushroom soup moistened with a little water, you will also pare the fixing time to about 5 minutes.

DELICATE MEATLOAF
BROWN RICE
TINY PEAS
SLICED CUCUMBERS WITH DILLED MAYONNAISE

DELICATE MEATLOAF

1½	lbs lean ground beef
1	egg, beaten
½	cup sour cream
8–10	saltines, crushed
3	scallions, finely chopped, green part and all
1	tablespoon Dijon mustard
	Salt and pepper to taste

Preheat oven to 350° F.

Combine all ingredients for meatloaf in a medium bowl. Transfer to a baking dish and form into a loaf. Put in oven.

Put a heavy saucepan of water on to boil for the brown rice. Add rice to boiling water, cover saucepan, and turn heat to very low. (Or cook rice according to directions on package.)

Fixing time: 15 minutes.

Relax for 45 minutes.

Return to the kitchen. Turn off heat under rice. Let meatloaf continue to cook as you prepare peas and salad.

Prepare peas according to package directions.

Peel and slice 2 cucumbers and put in a glass bowl. Add 2 squeezes of lemon juice and 3 tablespoons of mayonnaise. Mix thoroughly. Sprinkle with dried dill, salt, and pepper to taste. Mix again.

Remove meatloaf from oven. Drain peas and transfer to a serving dish; top with a teaspoon of butter. Bring everything to table. You're ready to eat.

Time from kitchen to table: 10 minutes.

Serves 4.

ZUCCHINI BOATS
CANTALOUPE SALAD

ZUCCHINI BOATS

- 1 large zucchini
- 1 lb ground beef or lamb
- 1 onion, finely chopped
- ½ green pepper, chopped
- 2 cloves garlic, minced
- 5 tablespoons oil
- 1 teaspoon Italian herb seasoning
- 1 teaspoon cinnamon
- ½ cup red wine
- ½ cup raisins
- ½ cup chopped walnuts
- 1 can (1 lb, 12 oz size) tomato puree
- 3 tablespoons honey

Preheat oven to 350° F.

Prepare boats: Slice zucchini in half lengthwise, scoop out inner pulp with a spoon, and discard. Place zucchini boats in well-oiled baking dish.

In a large skillet on top of stove, quickly sauté ground meat, onion, green pepper, and garlic in oil. Don't worry if meat is still pink; it will finish cooking in oven.

Add all spices and red wine. Mix well and simmer for 3 minutes. Add raisins and walnuts, and mix thoroughly. Remove skillet from heat.

Put meat mixture into zucchini boats. Pour tomato puree on top of meat mixture, letting excess partly fill baking dish. Dribble honey over top of zucchini boats. Place dish in oven, uncovered, and bake for 45 minutes to 1 hour.

Fixing time: about 15 minutes.

Relax for 45 minutes.

Return to the kitchen. Test zucchini for doneness by piercing with a fork. If tender, turn off heat and leave in oven while you make some rice and salad.

Serves 4.

CANTALOUPE SALAD

   1 small head Boston lettuce, washed, dried, and torn into pieces
   1 small cantaloupe, seeded and scooped into balls with
      melon-ball scooper

Dressing:
   ⅓ cup yogurt
   2 tablespoons lemon juice
   2 tablespoons mayonnaise
      Salt and pepper to taste

   Put lettuce and cantaloupe into a salad bowl and combine with dressing.
   Time from kitchen to table: 15 minutes.

PORK MENUS AND RECIPES

PORK CHOPS WITH PRUNES AND APRICOTS
LIMA BEANS, SQUASH, OR CORN
SALAD OF SLICED BEETS AND ONIONS

PORK CHOPS WITH PRUNES AND APRICOTS

   3 rib or loin pork chops, about ¾ inch thick
   9 pieces dried fruit (prunes, apricots, apples, or pears, or any
      combination of these)
 1½ cups water or apple juice
   ½ cup wine or fruit juice
      Salt and pepper

   Place pork chops in a greased skillet large enough so they do not overlap. Surround with dried fruit and add water or apple juice. Bring to a boil. Cover and lower heat so chops simmer.
   Fixing time: Under 5 minutes.
   Forget it for 45 minutes.
   Return to the kitchen. You should find pork chops tender and liquid just about evaporated. (If not, take out fruit and set aside. Boil up remaining liquid quickly.) Chops will be brown on the bottom side. Turn and brown other side in fat that remains in pan. Remove chops. Add wine or fruit juice to skillet and boil, scraping bottom of pan. Return chops and fruit to pan and simmer, covered, while fixing vegetable and making beet salad: Open and drain a can of sliced beets, add sliced onions to taste, and toss with oil and vinegar dressing.
   Time from kitchen to table: 10–15 minutes.
   Serves 3.

KIELBASA AND BEANS
SWEET-AND-SOUR CABBAGE

KIELBASA AND BEANS

>   One 1–1½-lb Kielbasa sausage ring
> 2 cloves garlic, finely chopped
> 2 cans (20-oz size) cannellini beans (white kidney beans)

Pierce sausage casing in several places and place in a large frying pan that has a cover. Put pan on top of the stove over medium heat.

While sausage is browning on one side, prepare Sweet-and-Sour Cabbage.

Chop garlic and add to frying pan.

Drain beans and put in a large sieve or colander. Rinse beans under cold running water.

Turn sausage, add beans to frying pan, and stir to mix with chopped garlic. Cover frying pan and turn down heat as low as you can.

Fixing time (for kielbasa, beans, and cabbage): less than 10 minutes. *Relax for 45 minutes.*

SWEET-AND-SOUR CABBAGE

> 1 small head cabbage (1–1½ lbs, or ½ large head)
> ½ cup white vinegar
> 1 tablespoon salt
> 3 tablespoons brown sugar
> 2 tablespoons butter
>   Pepper to taste

Wash and trim cabbage and cut into 8 wedge-shaped pieces.

Put 1 cup of water, vinegar, and salt in a heavy Dutch oven on top of stove over low heat. Add cabbage and cover. Return to kielbasa recipe. *Relax for 45 minutes.*

Return to the kitchen. Drain cabbage, return it to pot, and add brown sugar, butter, and pepper. Stir well, breaking up cabbage. Cover and let simmer as you fix remainder of meal.

Remove sausage to a large serving platter and cut into 3-inch pieces. Arrange beans around sausage. Bring everything to table.

Time from kitchen to table: 10 minutes.

Serves 4.

SAUERKRAUT WITH MEATS
RYE OR PUMPERNICKEL BREAD
MUSTARD
WHITE WINE OR BEER
FRUIT ICES OR SHERBET

SAUERKRAUT WITH MEATS (Choucroute Garnie)

- 2 lbs canned or fresh sauerkraut
  Strips of bacon or salt pork
- 1 medium onion, peeled
- 3 whole cloves
- 4 peppercorns
- 1 teaspoon caraway seeds (optional)
  White wine or beer
  Meats: frankfurters, knockwurst, pork chops, ham slices
  (use one or any combination)
- 2 large potatoes (optional)

Rinse sauerkraut and squeeze dry. Line a heavy pot with bacon or salt pork strips. Stud onion with cloves and place in pot with sauerkraut and seasonings. Pour in wine or beer almost to cover. Bring to a boil. Cover pot tightly and lower heat to a simmer.

Fixing time: less than 5 minutes.

Relax for 45 minutes.

When you're ready to assemble dinner, check sauerkraut; you may need to add a bit more liquid. Warm meats. If you're using frankfurters, simply bury them in simmering sauerkraut for 10 minutes. Knockwurst will take about 15 minutes. If you're serving ham slices, you can warm them quickly in wine or beer and then bury them for 5 minutes or so in sauerkraut. Pork chops, however, need to be part of mix from beginning. Brown them quickly in a skillet or under the broiler and put between layers of sauerkraut. If you like, you can at the same time pare two large potatoes, cut them in half, and bury them in the sauerkraut too.

Serve sauerkraut garnished with meat (choucroute garnie, as the French dub it) piping hot on a platter.

The sauerkraut can be cooked a day or even two days ahead and the meats added from time to time according to how much cooking they need.

Time from kitchen to table: 15–20 minutes.

Serves 4–5.

GLAZED PORK CHOPS AND BEANS
CHILLED APPLESAUCE
CRISP, CREAMY CUCUMBER SALAD
PUMPERNICKEL BREAD
ICE-COLD CIDER

GLAZED PORK CHOPS AND BEANS

> 2 tablespoons vegetable oil
> 6 center-cut pork chops
> 2 cans (28-oz size) pork and beans
> 2 tablespoons catsup
> 3–4 tablespoons brown sugar
> ½ teaspoon dry mustard

Preheat oven to 375° F.

Heat vegetable oil in a Dutch oven on top of the stove. Brown pork chops on both sides; remove pork and set aside. Discard grease. Pour beans into Dutch oven.

In a small bowl, mix catsup, brown sugar, dry mustard, and ¼ cup of water. Stir sauce into beans. Arrange pork chops on sauce and beans, and turn chops in sauce to coat both sides. Cover pan and put in oven.

Fixing time: about 10 minutes.

Relax for 45 minutes.

Return to the kitchen. Remove pan from oven. Test chops for doneness; a fork should pierce the meat easily. Spoon some sauce over chops. Return pan to oven. If chops are tender, turn off oven. If not, let them continue to cook until done.

Prepare the salad:

CRISP, CREAMY CUCUMBER SALAD

> 2 medium-size cucumbers, peeled and sliced
> 2 scallions, chopped (optional)
> ½ cup plain yogurt
> ½ cup mayonnaise
> Salt to taste
> Pepper to taste
> Garlic salt to taste

In a glass bowl, combine all ingredients. Put salad in refrigerator until dinner is ready.

When chops are done, take Dutch oven and salad to table. Chilled applesauce is a delicious addition to this satisfying meal.

Time from kitchen to table: 10 minutes.

Serves 4–6.

PORK CHOP DINNER IN ONE POT
SPINACH SALAD WITH CREAMY DRESSING
FRENCH BREAD
BEER OR
GRAPEFRUIT JUICE

PORK CHOP DINNER IN ONE POT

1½ tablespoons vegetable oil
4–5 medium-thick pork chops
   Flour
   Salt, pepper, poultry seasoning
1 medium-size sweet onion, cut into thick slices
1 green pepper, cut into rings
2 cups raw rice
1 large or 2 small tomatoes, skinned and sliced
2 cans (10½-oz size) beef or chicken consomme

This dish starts out on top of stove and ends up in oven. The beauty is that everything cooks in one big casserole, and there are no other pots or pans to use or clean up.

Preheat oven to 350° F.

Put oil in a heavy Dutch oven over medium heat. Lightly dust pork chops with flour and put in oil. Brown on both sides. Remove Dutch oven from heat. Sprinkle chops liberally with salt, pepper, and poultry seasoning. Put 1 thick slice of onion on each pork chop. Do same with pepper rings. Sprinkle rice over everything. Top rice with sliced tomatoes. Empty consomme into Dutch oven, making sure to distribute evenly. Cover casserole tightly and put in oven.

Fixing time: about 10 minutes.

Relax for one hour.

Return to the kitchen. Turn off oven and make salad. Spinach leaves could be prepared by your child or babysitter in the afternoon.

To dress salad, mix 1 part sour cream, 1 part plain yogurt, and 1 part mayonnaise with a squeeze of lemon juice and salt and pepper.

Pour dressing over spinach at the last minute, toss gently, and bring bowl right to table along with casserole and a loaf of crunchy French bread. You're ready for dinner.

Time from kitchen to table: 15 minutes.

Serves 4–5.

SMOTHERED PORK CHOPS
VEGETABLE SALAD
RYE BREAD

SMOTHERED PORK CHOPS

- 4 loin pork chops
- 8 new potatoes
- 2 cloves garlic
- 1 tablespoon oil
- 2½ cups white wine
- 1 package (16-oz size) sauerkraut, drained
-    Pepper to taste
- 2 teaspoons caraway seeds

Wipe chops with a paper towel. Scrub potatoes and pat dry. Chop garlic. Heat oil in a Dutch oven; sauté garlic until golden. Add chops and brown on both sides. Remove chops to a plate. Drain and discard oil from pan.

Add wine, sauerkraut, pepper, and caraway seeds to pan; stir well. Arrange chops and potatoes on sauerkraut and spoon liquid over them. Cover and cook over low-medium heat.

Fixing time: 15 minutes.

Relax for one hour.

Return to the kitchen. Turn off heat under pan but leave cover on.

Prepare vegetable salad: Peel a cucumber and slice into a salad bowl. Rinse some cherry tomatoes and add to bowl, along with a generous handful of bean sprouts. To make a creamy-tart dressing, combine ½ cup of sour cream, ¼ cup of buttermilk, 1 teaspoon of chopped chives, a squeeze of lemon juice, and dashes of salt and seasoned pepper. Toss salad with dressing. Arrange chops, potatoes, and sauerkraut on a large serving platter. You're ready for supper.

Time from kitchen to table: 15 minutes.

Serves 4.

PIQUANT PORK CHOPS
INSTANT MASHED POTATOES
ZESTY APPLESAUCE
TOMATO SALAD WITH OIL AND VINEGAR

PIQUANT PORK CHOPS

    4 medium-thick pork chops
      Flour for dredging
    2 tablespoons vegetable oil
    1 medium onion, sliced
    1 green pepper, seeded and sliced
      Dash of Worcestershire sauce
      Cayenne pepper to taste
      Salt and pepper to taste

Dredge pork chops in flour. Brown on both sides in oil in a large skillet over medium heat.

Arrange onion and pepper slices around and over the chops, add seasonings, and cover. Turn heat to low.

Fixing time: 10 minutes.

Relax for 45 minutes.

Return to the kitchen. Test chops for doneness. If they are easily pierced with a knife, turn off heat.

Empty a small jar of chilled applesauce into a small bowl and stir in 2 tablespoons or more of horseradish sauce.

Slice some tomatoes, arrange on a plate, and splash on a little oil and a tiny bit of vinegar. Add salt and pepper to taste.

Prepare instant mashed potatoes according to instructions on package. Turn potatoes into a serving dish and dot with butter.

Put chops on a platter, spoon onion and pepper mixture over them, and bring everything to table. You're ready to feast!

Time from kitchen to table: 10 minutes.

Serves 3–4.

PORK CHOPS PROVENÇALE
RICE
ROMAINE AND WALNUT SALAD

PORK CHOPS PROVENÇALE

- 4 pork chops
- Oil
- 1 can (28-oz size) whole peeled tomatoes with liquid
- 1 cup whole mushrooms
- 1 large onion, peeled and cut into eighths
- 2 green peppers, chopped
- 1 clove garlic, minced
- ½ teaspoon rosemary
- ½ teaspoon oregano
- Salt and pepper to taste

Preheat oven to 375° F.

In a Dutch oven over medium-high heat, brown chops in a little oil.

Add tomatoes and liquid, mushrooms, onion, peppers, garlic, rosemary, oregano, salt, and pepper. Bring to a boil. Cover and place in oven.

Fixing time: 15 minutes.

Relax for 45 minutes.

Return to the kitchen. Remove Dutch oven from oven. Turn pork chops and stir vegetables. Simmer, uncovered, on top of stove for 8–10 minutes. Meanwhile, prepare instant rice and this salad:

Wash some romaine and tear it into bite-size pieces. Pat or spin dry. Toss with Italian dressing and sprinkle on some chopped walnuts.

Spoon rice into center of a large platter. Transfer vegetables from Dutch oven with a slotted spoon and arrange them with chops around rice. Pour some sauce over rice and pour remainder into a small pitcher or creamer. Bring everything to table; you're ready to eat.

Time from kitchen to table: 10 minutes.

Serves 4.

PORK CHOPS WITH CABBAGE AND APPLES
BAKED SWEET POTATOES
TOMATOES VINAIGRETTE
WHITE WINE OR CIDER

PORK CHOPS WITH CABBAGE AND APPLES

    4 small sweet potatoes
    1 small head red or green cabbage
    2 small apples
      Butter or oil for browning
  4–5 medium-thick pork chops
    3 tablespoons Dijon mustard
    1 cup white wine
    1 cup apple juice
    1 tablespoon caraway seeds
      Salt and pepper to taste

Preheat oven to 350° F.

Scrub potatoes and prick several times with a fork. Put them in oven. Wash, core, and chop cabbage; core, pare, and thinly slice apples.

Heat butter or oil in a Dutch oven. Brown pork chops on both sides. Remove chops from Dutch oven to a plate; spread them on both sides with mustard. Pour wine and apple juice into Dutch oven; add caraway seeds, salt, and pepper. Bring quickly to a boil over medium heat. Turn off heat and return pork chops to Dutch oven; arrange cabbage and apples on top and around chops. Cover and put in oven.

Fixing time: about 15 minutes.

Relax for one hour.

Return to the kitchen. Check to see that chops and potatoes are done. If they're cooked through, turn off oven and prepare salad:

Wash and slice 4 medium tomatoes. Mix 2 parts oil to 1 part vinegar. Add a squeeze of lemon and salt and pepper. Pour dressing over tomato slices and toss. You're ready for supper.

Apples and apple juice give these pork chops a tangy sweet flavor. To make the dinner even sweeter, serve the buttered potatoes with a sprinkling of brown sugar.

Time from kitchen to table: 10 minutes.

Serves 4–5.

POULTRY MENUS AND RECIPES

CHICKEN PAPRIKA

RICE

PEAS, BROCCOLI SPEARS, GREEN BEANS, OR A

COMBINATION OF VEGETABLES SUCH AS

PEAS AND ONIONS

CHICKEN PAPRIKA

- 2 tablespoons butter or margarine
- ¼ cup chopped onion (frozen or fresh)
- 1 tomato (canned or fresh), peeled and chopped
- 1 teaspoon salt
- 1½ tablespoons paprika
- ¾ cup chicken broth or chicken stock, or 1 bouillon cube dissolved in ¾ cup water
  One 3-lb broiler/fryer, cut up or quartered
- 2 tablespoons flour
- ¼ cup water
- ½ cup sour cream

Melt butter in a skillet that has a tight cover. Add onion and sauté until it wilts. Add tomato, mashing it down with a fork or cutting it up with two knives. Add salt and paprika, stirring well, and then chicken broth. Bring to a boil. Add chicken pieces; turn over so they are coated by sauce on both sides. Cover skillet and lower flame.

Fixing time: 5–7 minutes.

Forget it for 40 minutes.

Return to the kitchen. Check chicken, and while it simmers about 5 minutes or more, prepare quick-cooking rice and frozen vegetable.

Mix flour and water; stir into chicken. Simmer for 3 minutes. At the last minute, stir in sour cream. Heat well but do not boil.

Time from kitchen to table: 10 minutes.

DREAMY CREAMY CHICKEN
BUTTERED PEAS
RICE
SLICED PEACHES WITH LEMON AND HONEY
ICED COFFEE OR MILK

DREAMY CREAMY CHICKEN

    1 can (10¾-oz size) cream of celery soup
    1 cup sour cream
    2 tablespoons vermouth, white wine, or sherry
    1 can (15½-oz size) boiled onions
 1½ lbs boneless, skinless chicken breasts
    ¼ cup grated Parmesan cheese

Preheat oven to 350° F.

Mix soup and sour cream with vermouth in a 1½-quart casserole with a lid, or a Dutch oven. Drain onions and stir gently into soup mixture.

Wash and dry chicken breasts and arrange them in casserole, pushing them down and spooning soup mixture over them. Sprinkle cheese over everything, cover, and put in oven.

Fixing time: 10 minutes.

Relax for 45 minutes.

Return to the kitchen. Test chicken for doneness; a sharp knife should pierce the meat easily. If chicken seems to be done, remove casserole from oven and keep warm.

Prepare frozen peas and rice according to package directions.

Peel and slice 4 fresh peaches and put in a glass bowl. Squeeze juice of ½ lemon over them and mix in 1–2 tablespoons of honey.

Time from kitchen to table: 15 minutes.

Serves 4.

CHICKEN TANDOORI
BROWN RICE
CUCUMBER, TOMATO, AND LETTUCE SALAD
COLD BEER OR HOT TEA
LEMON SHERBET

CHICKEN TANDOORI

    2 cups plain yogurt
 1½ teaspoons curry powder
       Juice of 1 lemon
       Salt and pepper to taste
    4 chicken breasts with skins, split

This chicken is tastiest when well marinated, so start preparing the night before you plan to serve it. In a medium bowl, combine yogurt, curry powder, lemon juice, salt, and pepper, and mix well. Arrange chicken in a single layer in a shallow baking dish. Pour mixture evenly over chicken, cover, and marinate in refrigerator overnight. If you have time the following morning, turn chicken pieces around in the marinade.

When you arrive home, preheat oven to 375° F and start water boiling for rice. Remove chicken from refrigerator and allow to stand at room temperature while oven is preheating.

Before placing chicken in oven, turn chicken skin-side up. Put in oven. Add rice to boiling water and cover tightly. Reduce heat as low as possible.

Fixing time: 5 minutes.

Relax for 45 minutes.

Return to the kitchen. Test chicken for doneness by piercing with a fork. If tender, turn off heat and leave in oven while you check rice and prepare salad. Slice cucumber and tomato; tear lettuce into small pieces. Sprinkle with fresh or dried dill and mix with oil and vinegar dressing.

If you like, you can spoon some fresh yogurt over chicken just before serving.

Time from kitchen to table: 10 minutes.

Serves 4–8.

CHICKEN MARENGO
ROMAINE AND CHICORY SALAD
FRENCH BREAD
WHITE WINE OR MILK

CHICKEN MARENGO

One 3½-lb frying chicken, cut up
1 tablespoon oil or butter
1 medium onion, sliced
1 clove garlic, minced
1 chicken bouillon cube
1 can (28-oz size) whole peeled tomatoes
1 bay leaf
1 teaspoon oregano
1 cup uncooked long-grain rice
  Salt and pepper to taste
1 red pepper, seeded and cut into strips, or 4 pimientos from a can
  or jar, cut into strips
1 jar (6-oz size) marinated artichoke hearts, drained

Preheat oven to 350° F.
Wash chicken and pat dry. Heat oil in a Dutch oven or casserole.
Place chicken in pan skin-side down and sauté over medium-high heat
until nicely browned.
Turn chicken pieces. Add onion and garlic; sauté for 5 minutes more.
Add 1 cup of boiling water, bouillon cube, tomatoes, bay leaf, and
oregano, and stir well. Bring to a boil. Stir in rice. Add salt and pepper
to taste. Cover casserole and place in oven.
Fixing time: 10 minutes.
Relax for 45 minutes.
Return to the kitchen. Remove casserole from oven. Arrange pepper
or pimiento slices and artichoke hearts on top, cover, and simmer on
top of stove for 5 minutes. While casserole is simmering, make the
salad.

ROMAINE AND CHICORY SALAD

1 large head romaine lettuce
1 small head chicory
½ cup diced celery
  Oil and vinegar dressing

Separate, wash, and drain romaine and chicory, and break into bite-size pieces. Place romaine, chicory, and celery in a large salad bowl. Toss with dressing.

Time from kitchen to table: 10 minutes.

Salad and casserole serve 4.

CHICKEN WITH DILL
LETTUCE AND CUCUMBER SALAD
CRUSTY BREAD
LEMONADE OR WHITE WINE

CHICKEN WITH DILL

- 1 medium green pepper
- 1 medium red pepper
- 1 medium zucchini
- 1 large onion
- 1 tablespoon oil
- 2 chicken breasts, split
- 1 tablespoon chopped fresh dill
- Salt and pepper

The sweet, crunchy peppers impart a light, tart flavor to chicken and, as it simmers, vegetable juices make it as tender as can be.

Coarsely chop peppers, slice zucchini, and quarter onion. Heat oil in a large skillet. Meanwhile, rinse chicken breasts and pat dry.

Quickly sauté chicken breasts in hot oil for several minutes, until golden on both sides. Add dill, salt, pepper, and all vegetables. Turn heat very low and cover skillet.

Fixing time: 15 minutes.

Relax for 45 minutes.

Return to the kitchen. Check chicken for doneness. A sharp knife should pierce meat easily. Remove from heat if tender, but leave cover on.

Prepare salad: Wash lettuce and pat or spin dry. Slice a cucumber. To make a creamy dressing, combine ⅔ cup of yogurt, ¼ cup of ricotta cheese, dashes of nutmeg, pepper, paprika, and vinegar, and 5 chopped mint leaves. Toss lettuce and cucumber with dressing. You're ready for supper.

Time from kitchen to table: 10 minutes.

Serves 4.

BAKED DEVILED CHICKEN
MANDARIN SALAD
RICE
PEAS

BAKED DEVILED CHICKEN

    3 lbs (6 pieces) chicken breasts
    4 tablespoons butter
    ½ cup honey
 ⅛–¼ cup yellow hot dog mustard
    1 teaspoon curry powder
    1 teaspoon salt

The beauty of this recipe is that you don't have to flour and brown chicken. The pungent sauce—which will fill your home with an incredible aroma—coats chicken and keeps it moist. Rice, peas, and a salad of mandarin oranges and greens are ideal accompaniments.

Preheat oven to 375° F.

Wash and skin chicken and dry each piece thoroughly with paper toweling. (You can substitute other chicken parts for breasts. If your family loves skin, leave it on, but reduce amount of butter to 2 tablespoons.)

Melt butter in a small saucepan. Turn off heat and mix in honey, mustard, curry powder, and salt.

Arrange chicken in one layer in a baking dish; pieces should be close but not overlapping.

Pour sauce over pieces. Turn once or twice to coat well. Leave breasts meaty side up and put dish in oven.

Fixing time: less than 10 minutes.

Relax for 45 minutes.

Return to the kitchen. Baste chicken with sauce. Continue to bake for 15 minutes more as you prepare rice, peas, and salad.

For an especially sparkling salad, try the following:

Pull apart, wash, and dry 1 small Boston lettuce and 1 small Bibb lettuce. Drain a can of mandarin oranges, or peel and section a seedless orange.

Combine lettuce and orange sections in a bowl and refrigerate. Then make this dressing:

Put in a blender 1 raw egg, ½ cup of salad oil, 2 tablespoons of wine vinegar, and a dash each of sugar, salt, and pepper. Mix well. Remove lettuce from refrigerator and combine with dressing when chicken is ready. Put chicken on a heated platter, leaving space at one end for rice and at the other end for peas.

Time from kitchen to table: 10–15 minutes.

Serves 4–6.

CRISPY GARLIC CHICKEN
BUTTERED RICE
BROCCOLI WITH CASHEWS

CRISPY GARLIC CHICKEN

>   One 3-lb broiler/fryer, cut up
>   Salt and pepper
>   Garlic powder
>   Paprika
> 1 large onion

This is the easiest chicken you'll ever make. And it's so delicious, you'll want to pick up the pieces in your fingers to get every last bit of tender meat and crisp, garlicky skin.

Preheat oven to 350° F.

Wash chicken pieces and pat dry with paper towels; put chicken on a sheet of waxed paper. Sprinkle each piece generously on both sides with salt, pepper, garlic powder, and paprika. With your fingers, rub seasonings into chicken.

Peel and slice onion and arrange slices on bottom of an ungreased casserole or baking dish. Arrange chicken pieces over onion slices and slide dish into oven.

Fixing time: 10 minutes.

Relax for one hour.

Return to the kitchen. Prepare rice and broccoli according to package directions. When rice is done, turn into a serving dish and mix in 1 tablespoon of butter.

When broccoli is done, drain thoroughly, turn into a serving dish, and carefully mix in about 1 handful of cashews. Squeeze ½ lemon over broccoli.

Check to see that chicken is done; a sharp knife should pierce the meat easily. If chicken is tender, remove from oven and arrange pieces on a serving platter. You're ready for supper.

Time from kitchen to table: 15 minutes.

Serves 4.

CHICKEN ELEGANTE
BUTTERED NOODLES
BROCCOLI
FRENCH BREAD
ORANGE-PINEAPPLE SHERBET

CHICKEN ELEGANTE

One 2½–3-lb chicken, cut up
¼ cup flour
1 teaspoon salt
2 tablespoons grated Parmesan or Romano cheese
4 tablespoons butter
1 can (15-oz size) artichoke hearts, drained
12 mushrooms
½ cup white wine
½ cup chicken broth

Preheat oven to 375° F.
Wash and dry chicken pieces. Put flour, salt, and cheese in a paper bag. Put 2 pieces of chicken at a time into bag; shake to coat with flour mixture.

Heat butter in a skillet over medium heat and brown chicken on all sides. Remove chicken pieces to a baking dish. Arrange artichoke hearts and mushrooms among chicken pieces. Pour wine and chicken broth into skillet; turn on heat for 1–2 minutes while you scrape bottom. Pour contents of skillet over chicken. Put chicken into oven uncovered.

Fixing time: 10 minutes.
Relax for 45 minutes.
Return to the kitchen. Test chicken for doneness; a sharp knife should easily pierce the meat.

Prepare noodles and broccoli according to package directions.
Time from kitchen to table: 15 minutes.
Serves 4.

CHICKEN DIJON
RICE
BEET, AVOCADO, AND RED ONION SALAD
FRENCH BREAD

CHICKEN DIJON

- 2 tablespoons butter or margarine
- 1 cup chopped onion
- 2 tablespoons Dijon mustard
- 1 teaspoon salt
- ¾ cup chicken broth or chicken stock, or 1 bouillon cube dissolved in ¾ cup water
  One 3-lb broiler/fryer, cut up or quartered
- ½ cup sour cream
- 1 small can sweet baby peas

Melt butter in a skillet that has a tight cover. Add onion and sauté until it wilts. Stir in mustard and salt, then add chicken broth and bring to a boil. Add chicken pieces; turn them over so they are coated by sauce on both sides. Cover skillet and turn heat down to low.

Fixing time: 10 minutes.

Relax for 45 minutes.

Return to the kitchen. Check chicken, and while it simmers about 5 minutes more, prepare rice and beet salad described below.

Stir sour cream and well-drained peas into chicken sauce. Simmer for 3 minutes but do not boil.

Serves 3–4.

BEET, AVOCADO, AND RED ONION SALAD

- 1 can (16-oz size) baby beets
- 1 avocado
- ½ sweet red onion
- 6 tablespoons olive oil
- 2 tablespoons vinegar
  Salt and freshly ground pepper to taste

Drain beets and place in a salad bowl. Peel and slice avocado. Peel and slice onion. Add both to salad bowl.

Combine oil, vinegar, salt, and pepper in a small jar with a tight cover and shake vigorously. Pour dressing over beet mixture and toss gently, taking care not to bruise avocado pieces.

Time from kitchen to table: 15 minutes.

SLEEPYTIME CHICKEN
RICE
SPARKLING GREEN SALAD
ICED TEA, LEMONADE, OR CHILLED WHITE WINE

SLEEPYTIME CHICKEN

Two 2½-lb fryers, cut up

Marinade:
- 1 cup dry vermouth
- 6 tablespoons soy sauce
- 2 tablespoons red wine vinegar
- 4 tablespoons sugar
- 2 garlic cloves, finely chopped
- 1 tablespoon ground ginger

This recipe is called "sleepytime" because you have to start marinating chicken the night before you plan to serve it. The next evening you will have one of the easiest dishes you will ever prepare. What's more, it's delicious enough to serve to guests—which is why this recipe calls for two chickens. (If you don't have company, keep second chicken to eat cold another night.)

The night before, mix marinade ingredients in a small bowl. Put chicken pieces into a large glass or ceramic bowl with marinade. Cover bowl with a plate and refrigerate.

The next evening, preheat oven to 325° F.

Remove chicken from marinade and arrange in 1 or 2 baking dishes so pieces don't touch. Put in oven.

Fixing time: 10 minutes.

Relax for 45 minutes.

Return to the kitchen. Remove chicken from oven, drain off fat, and turn pieces over. Brush chicken liberally with marinade and put remaining sauce in a pan over medium heat to serve later with rice.

Prepare rice according to directions on package.

Bake chicken about 10 minutes more, or until tender. Prepare salad.

SPARKLING GREEN SALAD

- 1 head Boston lettuce
- 2 scallions, chopped
- 3 tablespoons chopped parsley
  Italian dressing

Wash, dry, and tear lettuce into bite-size pieces. Put greens in a salad bowl and toss with bottled Italian dressing.

Time from kitchen to table: 10 minutes.

CHICKEN IN A DISH
(CHICKEN CUTLETS, ONION, AND RICE)
AVOCADO AND WATERCRESS SALAD
FRENCH BREAD
CIDER OR CHILLED WHITE WINE

CHICKEN IN A DISH

- 2 tablespoons vegetable oil
  Flour mixed with paprika to taste
- 6 chicken cutlets (3 breasts split)
- ½ large Spanish onion, chopped
- 1 heaping cup long-grain rice
- 2 cloves garlic, chopped
  Salt, pepper, poultry seasoning
- 1 can (13¾-oz size) or 2 cups chicken broth

Heat oil in a large skillet that has a cover. Flour cutlets and brown in hot oil. Add onion and sauté a bit longer. Push chicken and onion to sides of pan and put rice in center. Scatter chopped garlic and seasonings over everything and pour broth over rice. Cover skillet and reduce heat so chicken dish simmers.

Fixing time: under 15 minutes.

Forget it for 45 minutes.

Return to the kitchen. Lift cover and push rice into pockets of remaining liquid. Cover again and turn off heat.

As chicken and rice "set," wash and dry a bunch of watercress, peel and slice an avocado, and make a vinaigrette. (For latter, put 1 part wine vinegar and 4–5 parts salad oil in a jar with a cover. Add a dollop of Dijon mustard, salt, and pepper, and shake.) Combine salad and serve along with chicken, French bread, and cold drinks.

Time from kitchen to table: 10–15 minutes.

Serves 3–4.

BAKED MARINATED CHICKEN WITH
MUSHROOMS AND SCALLIONS
BROWN RICE
SALAD OF TOMATOES, LETTUCE, AND DILL

BAKED MARINATED CHICKEN

    1 broiler/fryer, quartered
    ½ cup soy sauce
      Juice of 1 lemon
    2 garlic cloves, chopped
    4 scallions, chopped
    8 mushrooms, halved
    2 cups uncooked brown rice

This dish is best when started the night before so chicken will be well marinated.

Place chicken in a bowl and combine with soy sauce, lemon juice, and garlic. Cover and refrigerate.

If you have time in the morning, turn pieces around in marinade.

When you come home in the evening, preheat oven to 350° F.

Arrange chicken in baking pan so pieces don't touch and pour marinade over them; place in oven.

Bring 3 cups of water and 1 teaspoon of salt to a boil. Add rice to boiling water. Cover tightly; reduce heat as low as possible. (If you use packaged brown rice, follow directions on box.)

Fixing time: about 5 minutes.

Relax for 45 minutes.

Return to the kitchen. Remove chicken from oven, turn pieces, and add a bit of water or white wine if necessary. Stir in scallions and mushrooms and return to oven for 5–10 minutes. Check rice; if water has been absorbed, turn off heat. If not, cover and cook until done.

Slice tomatoes and tear lettuce into pieces. Sprinkle with fresh or dried dill and mix with oil and vinegar dressing.

Note: If your family doesn't like mushrooms, substitute peas or baby carrots.

Time from kitchen to table: 5–10 minutes.

Serves 4.

TURKEY TETRAZZINI
WHOLE WHEAT ITALIAN BREAD
SPINACH, ZUCCHINI, AND CHERRY-TOMATO SALAD

TURKEY TETRAZZINI

- ¼ lb mushrooms
- 1 tablespoon butter
- 1½ cups turkey broth or gravy, or 1 can (14½-oz size) chicken broth
- ½ cup milk
- 3 tablespoons flour
  Salt and pepper to taste
- ½ teaspoon basil
- ½ lb thin spaghetti
- 1½ cups cubed leftover turkey
- ½ cup shredded mozzarella
- ¼ cup grated Parmesan cheese

As soon as you get home, put 2 quarts of salted water on to boil for spaghetti.

Preheat oven to 350° F.

Wash and slice mushrooms. Heat butter in a medium saucepan. Sauté mushrooms until golden. Add turkey broth and bring to a boil. Remove from heat.

Put milk and flour in a small jar with a lid (if using gravy, only 1 tablespoon of flour is needed). Shake until there are no flour lumps. Stir milk mixture into broth or gravy. Cook over medium heat, stirring constantly, until thickened. Add salt and pepper to taste. Stir in basil.

Cook spaghetti according to package directions. Drain and return to pot. Pour half of sauce over spaghetti; toss until well coated. Turn into greased 2-quart baking dish. Stir turkey into remaining sauce; spoon over spaghetti. Sprinkle casserole with mozzarella and Parmesan cheese. Place in oven.

Fixing time: 10 minutes.

Relax for 45 minutes.

Return to the kitchen. If casserole is nicely browned, turn off oven.

To make salad, break ½ lb of prewashed spinach into a salad bowl; remove tough stems. Wash and thinly slice 1 small zucchini. Wash 12 cherry tomatoes. Add zucchini and tomatoes to spinach. Toss with Italian dressing.

Casserole and salad serve 4.

Time from kitchen to table: 10 minutes.

CHAPTER TWO
YOU START THE DINNER, AND I'LL FINISH WHEN I GET HOME

One of the hardest things to face after a long day at work is the dash into the kitchen to fix dinner while everybody hovers expectantly around the table. Yet in most families someone is home before Mom or Dad is and could very well get the meal started. If there are very young children, there may be a sitter. Children old enough to care for themselves after school are old enough to cook and probably would love to. A teenager or a husband who gets home early could have dinner simmering by the time you arrive. To all these helpers, this Start the Dinner section is dedicated.

A teenager, a baby-sitter, or a husband should be able to prepare these recipes with very little help, but a preteen might want to read the recipes the night before in order to question anything not understood. Unless they are very experienced cooks, we suggest devoting a little time over the weekend to a kitchen tour so they can locate kitchen equipment, identify each item, and learn what it is used for. Make sure that everyone knows where to find all the staples as well.

Go over safety rules and point out things that should not be touched. Encourage the use of hand tools, such as a rotary eggbeater or wire whisk, rather than an electric mixer. Do not let children use a blender, processor, or sharp knives when you are not at home. A vegetable peeler or a small serrated knife can be used for peeling and cutting.

Don't assume anything. Some procedures are so basic that many cookbooks take them for granted; for example, that you should wash vegetables and fruits and remove the papery outer layer from onions and garlic before using them, or that it's all right for some leaves to remain on the celery when you cook it but not on the rhubarb.

Each of the following menus includes directions for starting the main part of the meal; they are planned so that dinner is served at 6:30.

The menus include easy-to-prepare salads that Mother can make just before serving time. Breads and desserts can be family favorites right from the supermarket. Or, on days when schedules permit, children may prepare one of our delicious "Bake Along with Dinner" desserts as an alternate to the dessert in the menu.

BARBECUED BEEF ROAST AND BAKED POTATOES
SOUR CREAM DRESSING
BUTTERED PEAS AND CARROTS
MIXED GREEN SALAD
WHOLE WHEAT LOAF
ICE CREAM WITH CHOCOLATE SYRUP
COFFEE, TEA, OR MILK

BARBECUED BEEF ROAST AND BAKED POTATOES

    One 4–5-lb beef chuck roast
1 can (10¾-oz size) condensed onion soup
½ cup catsup
½ teaspoon chili powder
4–6 medium baking potatoes (2½–3 lbs)

3:50—Preheat oven to 375° F. Wipe roast well with damp paper towels. Place roast in a Dutch oven. Add ¾ cup of water, onion soup, and catsup. Turn roast around several times in mixture. Sprinkle with chili powder. Cover and place in oven. Bake for 2½ hours.

4:50—Scrub potatoes under cold running water. Let drain on paper towels. Prick skins several times with a fork. Place potatoes right on oven rack, being careful not to touch any part of oven. Bake 1¼–1½ hours, or until potatoes feel soft when pierced with a fork.

That does it; you're finished. Let mom or dad do the rest.

6:05—Assemble salad and refrigerate. Prepare sour cream dressing: Mix together 1 cup of sour cream, 2 tablespoons of chopped parsley, 2 chopped scallions, and ¼ teaspoon of dried dill weed. Cook frozen peas and carrots.

6:20—Remove potatoes from oven. Slash an X in the top of each potato. Then, holding potato with pot holders, squeeze ends so steam can escape and potato fluffs up. Remove roast to a serving platter. Slice across grain into very thin slices. Skim fat from liquid in Dutch oven; pour liquid into a gravy boat and serve with beef. Serve sour cream dressing with potatoes.

Makes 4–6 servings, with 4 servings left for another meal.

6:30—*Dinner is served.*

MEATLOAF EN CROUTE
BAKED VEGETABLE CASSEROLE
PEACH AND CRANBERRY SALAD
BROWNIES
COFFEE, TEA, OR MILK

MEATLOAF EN CROUTE

1½ lbs ground chuck
  2 eggs
¾ cup raw quick-cooking oats
  1 can (8-oz size) stewed tomatoes
¼ cup (½ package of 1⅜-oz size) dehydrated onion soup mix
  1 package (8-oz size) refrigerator crescent dinner rolls

BAKED VEGETABLE CASSEROLE

  1 package (10-oz size) frozen baby lima beans
  1 package (10-oz size) frozen corn kernels
½ teaspoon salt
¼ teaspoon dried thyme
     Dash of pepper
  1 tablespoon butter
  1 can (3-oz size) French-fried onions

5:10—Preheat oven to 375° F. Grease a 9-by-5-by-3-inch loaf pan. In a medium bowl, stir together ground chuck, eggs, oats, tomatoes, and onion soup mix until well combined. Turn into loaf pan; pat top to make level. Place in oven. Set timer for 50 minutes.

5:50—Prepare vegetable casserole: Pour lima beans into a 1-quart shallow baking dish. Pour corn over top. Sprinkle with salt, thyme, and pepper. Gently add ¼ cup of water. Using a butter knife, cut butter into small cubes and add to top of casserole. Cover tightly and place in oven at 6:00. Bake for 30 minutes.

That does it; you're finished. Let mom or dad do the rest.

6:10—When timer rings, remove meatloaf from oven. Carefully pour off liquid, loosen edges, and turn out onto baking pan or ovenproof serving platter. Open tube of rolls; separate and arrange on top and sides of loaf. Return to oven and bake 12–15 minutes, or until rolls are golden brown. Prepare salad: Arrange peach halves and whole-berry cranberry sauce on lettuce.

Remove vegetable casserole from oven. Top with onion rings.

Makes 6 servings.

6:30—*Dinner is served.*

GLAZED PORK CHOPS WITH APPLES
BAKED ACORN SQUASH
BUTTERED GREEN BEANS
MIXED GREEN SALAD WITH ALFALFA SPROUTS
WARM CORN MUFFINS
FROZEN YOGURT
COFFEE, TEA, OR MILK

GLAZED PORK CHOPS WITH APPLES

  6 rib pork chops, ½ inch thick
  ½ teaspoon marjoram
  1 teaspoon salt
  ¼ teaspoon pepper
  1 can (21-oz size) apple pie filling

BAKED ACORN SQUASH

2–3 medium acorn squash
     Butter
     Brown sugar

4:50—Preheat oven to 375° F. Wipe pork chops with damp paper towels. Arrange in 2-quart covered casserole. Add ¼ cup of water. Sprinkle with marjoram, salt, and pepper. Top with pie filling. Cover and bake for 1½ hours.

5:20—Scrub squash. Set in shallow baking dish. Bake for 1 hour, or until soft when pierced with a fork.

That does it; you're finished. Let mom or dad do the rest.

6:20—Prepare salad and refrigerate. Cook frozen green beans. Wrap corn muffins in foil and place in oven to warm. Remove squash from oven. Cut each in half, and scoop out and discard seeds. Top each half with ½ teaspoon of butter and 1 teaspoon of brown sugar.

Makes 4–6 servings.

6:30—*Dinner is served.*

HAMBURGERS IN BUNS
BAKED MACARONI AND CHEESE
BUTTERED BROCCOLI
SLICED TOMATOES WITH DILL
FRESH FRUIT
COFFEE, TEA, OR MILK

BAKED MACARONI AND CHEESE

1 package (8-oz size) high-protein macaroni, elbow macaroni, shells, or other small pasta
Salt
Butter
1 cup milk
2 tablespoons flour
1 package (4-oz size) grated cheddar cheese

5:00—Preheat oven to 375° F. Pour 1 quart of water into deep 1½-quart casserole. Add macaroni, ½ teaspoon of salt, and 1 teaspoon of butter. Stir, cover tightly, and place in oven. Set time for 35 minutes.

5:35—Remove casserole from oven. Carefully pour macaroni into colander to drain, then return to casserole. Measure milk, flour, and ¼ teaspoon of salt into a 2-cup jar. Cover and shake until well combined. Pour over macaroni. Stir ½ of cheese into macaroni mixture. Sprinkle remainder on top. Return to oven until mixture bubbles and is thickened, about 20–25 minutes.

That does it; you're finished. Let mom or dad do the rest.

6:00—Slice tomatoes, sprinkle with dill weed, cover, and refrigerate. Cook frozen broccoli. Prepare hamburgers using your favorite method.

6:15—Turn off oven. Leave macaroni in oven to stay warm until serving time.

Makes 4–6 servings.

6:30—*Dinner is served.*

PORK WITH BEANS
PINEAPPLE COLESLAW
BRAN MUFFINS
VANILLA ICE CREAM

PORK WITH BEANS

> One 3-lb cooked, smoked, boneless pork butt
> 2 cans (20¾-oz size) baked beans
> 1 cup apple juice or water

4:30—Preheat oven to 350° F. Remove wrappings from pork butt. Place pork in a medium-size Dutch oven. Open beans and pour over the pork along with apple juice. Cover pan and place in hot oven.

To start pineapple coleslaw, open 1 can (8-oz size) crushed pineapple. Put pineapple with its juice into a large bowl. Stir in ½ cup of mayonnaise and ¼ teaspoon of celery seeds, if you have them. Peel off and discard tough outer leaves of a medium-size head of cabbage. Rinse well and drain. Put bowl of pineapple dressing and cabbage in refrigerator.

That does it; you're finished. Let mom or dad do the rest.

6:00—Open a package of bran muffins and put them in oven to warm.

To finish coleslaw, shred cabbage by hand or in a food processor and toss with chilled dressing. Remove muffins and pork from oven. Arrange muffins in a serving basket. Bring everything to table. Slice pork and serve with baked beans right from Dutch oven.

Serves 6.

6:15—*Dinner is served.*

SMOKED PORK AND SAUERKRAUT
PINEAPPLE SALAD

SMOKED PORK AND SAUERKRAUT

     One 3-lb fully cooked, smoked, boneless pork-shoulder butt
  2 cans (1-lb size) or 2 bags (1-lb size) fresh sauerkraut
 12 small carrots
  6 medium potatoes

     4:00—Preheat oven to 350° F. Remove wrapping from pork butt. Rinse and place in a 5-quart Dutch oven. Open sauerkraut and pour around pork in Dutch oven. Add 1 cup of water. Place Dutch oven on stove over medium heat and bring sauerkraut mixture to a boil. Turn off heat.

While waiting for sauerkraut mixture to boil, peel carrots and potatoes with a vegetable peeler. Add to Dutch oven, cover with a tight lid and, using pot holders, place in oven. (Be careful: Both are now hot.)

Start salad: Open 1 can (8-oz size) pineapple chunks. Drain juice into a cup. In a bowl, mix ½ cup of mayonnaise, pineapple chunks, 2 tablespoons of pineapple juice, and ¼ cup raisins. Place bowl in refrigerator. Wash 2 apples; they'll be added to salad later. Set leftover juice aside for use at another time.

That does it; you're finished. Let mom or dad do the rest.

6:00—Check Dutch oven to see if mixture needs more liquid. If necessary, add a little water and return to oven to keep warm. Slice unpeeled apples and toss with pineapple-raisin mixture. Serve salad from bowl or turn out onto a plate lined with lettuce. Warm some Kaiser rolls or a loaf of unsliced whole wheat bread. Slice smoked pork and serve from Dutch oven. Serves 6.

6:20—*Dinner is served.*

BAKED STUFFED PEPPERS WITH TOMATO SAUCE
SPINACH AND 3-BEAN SALAD

BAKED STUFFED PEPPERS WITH TOMATO SAUCE

- 4 large green peppers
- 1 lb ground beef
- ¾ cup quick-cooking rice
- 1 teaspoon chopped dehydrated onion
- ½ teaspoon salt
- ½ teaspoon basil
- 1 can (6-oz size) mixed vegetable juice
- 1 can (16-oz size) stewed tomatoes
- ½ cup shredded cheddar or Muenster cheese

SPINACH AND 3-BEAN SALAD

- 1 package (10-oz size) prewashed spinach
- 1 jar (18-oz size) 3-bean salad
- 4 tablespoons bottled Italian dressing

4:30—Wash peppers and trim off tops. Remember to cut away from your hand. Scoop out seeds and membrane. Set upright in a deep 3-quart casserole or soufflé dish.

In a large bowl, mix together ground beef, rice, onion, salt, basil, vegetable juice, and 1 cup of stewed tomatoes. Stir with a fork until tomatoes are broken up and everything is well combined. Spoon mixture into peppers. Pour remaining stewed tomatoes around peppers. Cover tightly with a lid or foil. Set in oven; close door and turn oven on to 350° F.

Carefully rinse spinach in a colander. Break off any tough stems. Set colander in a bowl or pie plate and place in refrigerator. Put jar of 3-bean salad in refrigerator to chill.

That does it; you're finished. Let mom or dad do the rest.

6:00—Remove lid or foil from peppers. Sprinkle cheese over tops of peppers and return to oven. Place rolls or bread in oven. Turn off heat. Break spinach into salad bowl. Drain 3-bean salad and add to spinach. Pour dressing over salad and toss.

When cheese is melted and rolls or bread is warm, dinner is ready. Serves 4.

6:15—Dinner is served.

ROAST LEG OF LAMB WITH VEGETABLES
MINT JELLY
LETTUCE AND TOMATO SALAD

ROAST LEG OF LAMB WITH VEGETABLES

    One 5-lb leg of lamb
1 clove garlic
1 teaspoon salt
$\frac{1}{8}$ teaspoon pepper
$\frac{1}{2}$ teaspoon dried rosemary leaves
4 (about 2 lbs) large baking potatoes
4 (about $\frac{1}{2}$ lb) large carrots
4 (about 1 lb) medium onions
1 tablespoon butter

3:30—Wipe lamb with damp paper towels. Place fat-side up on rack in shallow roasting pan. Peel garlic and carefully cut into 4 pieces. With a paring knife, cut 4 slits in top of lamb. Be sure to cut away from your hand. Stick a piece of garlic into each slit. Sprinkle lamb with salt and pepper. Crumble rosemary over top. Place in oven, close door, and set oven at 325° F.

Wash potatoes and carrots; peel with a vegetable peeler. Peel onions and rub some butter on each one.

4:00—Open oven door. Carefully place vegetables in pan; arrange around lamb, with carrots on bottom. Close oven door.

That does it; you're finished. Let mom or dad do the rest.

6:00—Turn potatoes; insert meat thermometer into lamb. If carrots and onions are tender, remove and keep warm. Return meat and potatoes (and other vegetables, if they're not yet tender) to oven until thermometer registers desired degree of doneness—150° F for rare and 175° F for medium. Make salad.

Remove lamb and vegetables to platter. Garnish with mint jelly.

Serves 4.

6:20—*Dinner is served.*

ROBUST POT ROAST
GRAVY
NOODLES
SALAD

ROBUST POT ROAST

    Flour
    One 3-lb rump roast
3 tablespoons vegetable oil
1 can (16-oz size) stewed tomatoes
1 can onion soup
8 carrots

3:00—Preheat oven to 325° F. Put ¼ cup of flour on a plate; turn roast in flour until coated on all sides. Put a Dutch oven over medium heat and add oil. When it is hot, carefully place roast in pot. Brown meat on all sides. Turn off heat.

Open stewed tomatoes and onion soup, and pour both into Dutch oven. Peel carrots and add to mixture. Cover pot and put in oven.

That does it; you're finished. Let mom or dad do the rest.

6:00—Remove pot from oven and test meat with a fork. If fork pierces meat with relative ease, meat is done. In that case, remove meat and carrots to a plate and skim fat from liquid. Put Dutch oven over medium heat and bring liquid (including tomato pieces) to a boil. (If meat is still tough, cook 15–20 minutes more on top of the stove over medium heat.)

Mix 3 tablespoons of flour with 1 cup of water and add to cooking liquid. Stir well and turn heat down to a very low setting.

Put a saucepan of water on to boil for noodles. Slice roast with a very sharp knife. Put meat slices and carrots back into Dutch oven to continue cooking with gravy for about 10 minutes.

Meanwhile, cook noodles and assemble salad.

This meal should serve a family of 4 at least twice.

6:20—*Dinner is served.*

POACHED CHICKEN
CORN AND LIMA BEANS
GRAVY
SALAD

POACHED CHICKEN

    One 3-lb ready-to-cook broiler/fryer
  1 teaspoon salt
    Dash of pepper
  ¼ teaspoon dried thyme
  1 package (16-oz size) frozen corn kernels
  1 package (10-oz size) frozen baby lima beans

5:00—Preheat oven to 375° F. Remove giblets from chicken and rinse giblets and chicken well under running water. Let drain. Place chicken in a Dutch oven. Sprinkle with salt, pepper, and thyme. Pour 1¼ cups of water around chicken. Add giblets, cover pan, and put in oven. Set timer for 45 minutes.

6:00—When timer rings, remove Dutch oven to top of stove. Uncover and pour corn around chicken. Pour lima beans on top of corn. Return Dutch oven to oven. Set timer for 20 minutes.

That does it; you're finished. Let mom or dad do the rest.

6:15—Prepare salad and refrigerate. When timer rings, turn off oven and remove Dutch oven. Uncover and carefully remove chicken and vegetables (using a meat fork and a slotted spoon) to a serving platter. Cover with foil and return to oven to keep warm. Wrap rolls in foil and place in oven. To make gravy, put Dutch oven on top of stove over medium heat. Measure ½ cup of water and 3 tablespoons of flour into a small jar with a tight-fitting lid. Cover and shake until well combined. Stir into broth in Dutch oven until liquid thickens. Makes 4–6 servings.

6:30—*Dinner is served.*

HEARTY BEEF STEW
LETTUCE AND CHERRY-TOMATO SALAD
PUMPERNICKEL BREAD
APPLESAUCE WITH NUTMEG

HEARTY BEEF STEW

- 2½ lbs beef chuck, cut into 2-inch cubes
- 1 can (10½-oz size) condensed beef broth
- ½ teaspoon salt
- ¼ teaspoon pepper
- ½ teaspoon thyme
- 1 dried bay leaf
- 8 large carrots
- 8 medium potatoes
- 16 small white onions

4:00—Put beef cubes in a 4-quart Dutch oven with an oven-proof cover. Open beef broth and pour over meat. Fill can with water and add to Dutch oven along with salt, pepper, thyme, and bay leaf. Put on lid and set pan in oven. Turn on oven to 350° F.

Wash vegetables. Using a vegetable peeler, peel carrots and potatoes. Rinse and put in a big bowl.

Hold onions under warm running water and pull off outer skins. Put onions in bowl with other vegetables and cover with plastic wrap.

Separate leaves from a head of Boston lettuce. Wash each leaf carefully and drain lettuce well in a colander or dry in a salad spinner. Break lettuce into bite-size pieces and put in a salad bowl. Place bowl in refrigerator.

That does it; you're finished. Let mom or dad do the rest.

6:00—Remove meat from oven. Split carrots in half lengthwise. Cut potatoes in quarters. Add carrots, potatoes, and onions to meat in Dutch oven and place on top of stove. Cook stew gently until vegetables are tender—20–30 minutes. Stir occasionally and add water or wine if liquid is too low. If you want to thicken juices, stir 2 tablespoons of flour into ½ cup of water and gently stir into stew. Bring to bubbling and cook 5 minutes more.

Remove salad bowl from refrigerator. Wash 12 cherry tomatoes and add to lettuce. Toss with favorite bottled dressing.

6:30—*Dinner is served.*

ROAST PORK WITH YAMS
GREEN BEANS
CHUNKY APPLESAUCE

ROAST PORK WITH YAMS

One 5-lb bone-in fresh pork shoulder, or ½ fresh ham
1 large onion
1 teaspoon salt
¼ teaspoon pepper
½ teaspoon dried basil leaves
4 large yams (about 2 lbs)
4 teaspoons butter

3:15—Preheat oven to 375° F. Wipe pork with damp paper towels. Place in a roasting pan. Remove skin from onion. Cut it in half, being careful to cut away from your hand. Turn so that cut side is down on a cutting board. Slice each half into 4 pieces. Place on pork. Sprinkle with salt, pepper, and basil. Cover tightly with ovenproof lid or aluminum foil. Place in oven carefully—oven will now be hot.

Scrub yams well. Rinse in cold water. Prick skins several times on the top. Set aside at room temperature. Open jar of applesauce and divide it into fruit dishes. Sprinkle each serving with some cinnamon or prepared cinnamon-sugar mixture. Place them in refrigerator.

4:15—Open oven door, being careful to stay back until first wave of heat has rushed out. Then carefully set yams right on oven rack. Close oven and reduce heat to 350° F.

That does it; you're finished. Let mom or dad do the rest.

6:00—Remove cover from pork. Insert meat thermometer. Return roast to oven until surface is browned and thermometer registers 180° F.

Rinse a pound of green beans; cut off stem ends. Place beans in a heavy, medium-size saucepan with just enough water to cover. Sprinkle with salt. Cook covered for about 8 minutes, or until beans are just tender. Drain and toss with a little butter. Arrange pork and yams on a serving platter. Cut an X in top of each yam. Put a dot of butter in cut. Remove applesauce from refrigerator.

This meal should serve a family of 4, with meat left over for a second meal.

6:25—*Dinner is served.*

SPARERIBS WITH SAUERKRAUT
CUCUMBERS IN SOUR CREAM
PAPRIKA POTATOES
WARM RYE LOAF
APPLES AND CHEDDAR CHEESE
COFFEE OR CIDER

SPARERIBS WITH SAUERKRAUT

- 4 lbs spareribs or country-style ribs
- 2 packages (16-oz size) fresh sauerkraut
- 1 cup apple juice
- 1 tablespoon caraway seeds

3:30—Put spareribs in a large Dutch oven. Drain sauerkraut and place in a large bowl. Add apple juice and caraway seeds; stir to mix into sauerkraut. Add sauerkraut mixture to ribs. Cover Dutch oven, set it in oven, and turn on heat to 350° F.

Wash 4 potatoes and peel, using a vegetable peeler. Put in a bowl, cover with water, and set aside.

Wash 4 apples. Remove wedge of cheddar cheese from refrigerator. Arrange apples and cheese on a board or platter, ready to serve at dessert time.

That does it; you're finished. Let mom or dad do the rest.

6:00—Cut potatoes into quarters. Cook in enough boiling water to cover for 20–25 minutes. Put bread in oven to warm.

Peel and slice 2 cucumbers and put in a salad bowl. Add 2 table-spoons of mayonnaise, ½ cup of sour cream, and some dried dill. Toss together until cucumbers are well coated.

Drain potatoes and turn into a serving bowl. Add some butter and sprinkle with paprika. Remove spareribs, sauerkraut, and bread from oven. You're ready to eat!

The spareribs will serve a family of 4 with enough left over for the next day.

6:30—*Dinner is served.*

SWISS STEAK
BUTTERED NOODLES
COLESLAW
RASPBERRY SHERBET

SWISS STEAK

  1 lb shoulder steak or round steak, about 1 inch thick
     Flour for dredging
     Vegetable oil
  2 small onions
  2 cans (1-lb size) stewed tomatoes
  2 tablespoons tapioca
     Beef broth, red wine, or water (if additional liquid is needed)

4:00—Unwrap meat and place on a big plate. Sprinkle about 1 tablespoon of flour over it and press flour into one side of steak. Turn meat over and repeat with more flour.

Put a big skillet (that has a cover) on top of the stove over medium heat. (You could also use a Dutch oven.) Add about 2 tablespoons of oil. When it is hot, shake excess flour off meat and put in skillet. Brown steak on both sides.

Peel onions and slice carefully. The slices don't have to be very thin. Add to skillet and let them brown a bit around steak. If there isn't enough room, remove meat, brown onions, then put meat back. Open tomatoes and pour over meat. Stir tapioca into tomatoes.

Cover pan and turn heat down low.

That does it; you're finished. Let mom or dad do the rest.

5:30—Check meat, adding salt and pepper to taste. Add a little liguid if there isn't enough. Cover and continue to cook.

Prepare noodles according to directions on package. While noodles cook, make some coleslaw.

Serves 4.

6:00—*Dinner is served.*

CRACKED WHEAT PILAF
MEATBALLS PAPRIKASH
SLICED TOMATOES

CRACKED WHEAT PILAF

- 1 clove garlic
- 1 cup cracked wheat
- ½ teaspoon salt
- 1 tablespoon butter

MEATBALLS PAPRIKASH

- 1 lb ground chuck
- ¼ teaspoon salt
- ¼ cup uncooked oatmeal
- 1 envelope onion soup mix
- 1 egg
- 2 tablespoons butter
- 1 teaspoon paprika
- 2 tablespoons flour
- 1 cup sour cream

4:00—Start Cracked Wheat Pilaf: Measure 3 cups of water into a medium saucepan. Place over medium heat and bring to a boil. Crush garlic slightly with a butter knife or back of a spoon; peel off outer covering and discard it. Add garlic to water along with cracked wheat and salt. Remove pan from heat. Cover and set aside.

5:00—Make Meatballs Paprikash: In a large bowl, lightly toss ground chuck with salt, oatmeal, 1 tablespoon of onion soup mix (save remaining mix for later), and egg until well combined. Gently shape meat mixture into 16 balls. Heat butter in a large skillet on top of stove over medium heat. Add meatballs and brown well on all sides. Combine 1 cup of water, paprika, and remainder of onion soup mix in a small bowl. Add to pan. Bring meatballs and sauce to a boil, cover, and reduce heat to low. Turn off heat after 10 minutes and leave pan there.

That does it; you're finished. Let mom or dad do the rest.

6:00—Stir flour into ¼ cup of water until smooth. Add to meatball mixture. Turn heat to medium under pan. Simmer, stirring, until thickened and smooth. Place saucepan containing cracked wheat over medium heat. Bring to a boil, stirring occasionally. Drain well; remove garlic and stir in butter. Turn onto serving platter. Wash and slice tomatoes, and arrange on another platter. Drizzle with bottled dressing. Fold sour cream into meatball mixture and heat gently. Do not boil. Spoon meatballs and sauce onto pilaf.

Serves 4.

6:20—*Dinner is served.*

OLD-FASHIONED MEATLOAF
BAKED POTATOES
SLICED CUCUMBERS VINAIGRETTE
CHOCOLATE ICE CREAM

OLD-FASHIONED MEATLOAF

- 1 small onion
- 1½ lbs ground beef
- 1 egg, beaten
- ½ cup bread crumbs
- 1 tablespoon grated Parmesan cheese
- 1 teaspoon oregano
- 1 tablespoon dried parsley
- 1 teaspoon salt
- ¼ teaspoon pepper
- 1 can (8-oz size) tomato sauce

4:45—Preheat oven to 350° F. Carefully peel and chop onion. In a large mixing bowl, combine onion, beef, egg, bread crumbs, cheese, oregano, parsley, salt, and pepper. Add ½ of tomato sauce. Mix gently with your hands. Put meat mixture into a 9-by-5-by-3-inch loaf pan and press down gently to fill pan. Pour remainder of tomato sauce over top of meatloaf. Carefully slide pan into hot oven.

5:15—Scrub 4 potatoes; prick each about 6 times with a fork. Open oven carefully and place potatoes on rack next to meatloaf pan.

That does it; you're finished. Let mom or dad do the rest.

6:10—Peel and thinly slice 2–3 cucumbers; arrange slices on a plate and drizzle with oil and vinegar dressing. Remove meatloaf and potatoes from oven. Use a spatula to remove meatloaf to a serving platter.

Serves 4.

6:20—*Dinner is served.*

BEEF AND BARLEY SOUP
HOT FRENCH BREAD WITH HERB BUTTER
LETTUCE AND TOMATO SALAD
CHOCOLATE ICE CREAM
SUGAR COOKIES

BEEF AND BARLEY SOUP

½ lb beef (or lamb) cubes
2 tablespoons instant minced onion
½ teaspoon basil
1 teaspoon salt
1 cup hulled barley
1 package (10-oz size) frozen peas and carrots, or 1 bunch fresh carrots, scraped and cut into 2-inch pieces

4:00—Measure 6 cups of water into a large, heavy pot. If meat cubes are larger than 1 inch square, cut in half with kitchen scissors. Add meat, onion, basil, and salt to water; stir to mix ingredients. Over high heat, bring water to a boil, then reduce heat until soup is cooking gently. Cover pot.

Wash ½ head of lettuce, tear into pieces, and dry with paper toweling; put into a salad bowl. Wash 8 cherry tomatoes and remove stems; put tomatoes into bowl. If your family likes black olives, open a small can, drain well, and add to salad; place salad in refrigerator.

5:00—Turn off heat under soup and carefully remove lid so steam comes out away from you. Add 1 cup of cold water. Put barley in a colander and run cold water over it, then slowly pour barley into pot. Turn heat under soup to high and keep cooking until soup is boiling; reduce heat and cover pot. Take a stick of butter out of refrigerator to soften.

That does it; you're finished. Let mom or dad do the rest.

6:00—Skim fat off soup. Stir frozen peas and carrots or fresh carrots into soup; cook gently until vegetables are tender. Adjust seasoning. Preheat broiler. Combine ½ stick of butter with 1 teaspoon of chopped parsley or dill in a small bowl. Split a loaf of French bread and spread with herb butter. Broil for several minutes until golden. Toss salad with your favorite dressing.

Serves 3.

6:30—*Dinner is served.*

STUFFED ROAST CHICKEN
CRANBERRY SAUCE
BROCCOLI WITH LEMON BUTTER

STUFFED ROAST CHICKEN

One 4–5 lb roasting chicken
5 slices bread
1 tablespoon instant minced onion
½ teaspoon dried basil leaves
1 can (10¾-oz size) condensed chicken broth
1 tablespoon butter, softened
½ teaspoon herb-seasoning salt
4–6 medium baking potatoes
¼ cup flour

4:00—Preheat oven to 350° F. Remove wrapping from chicken. Wipe outside and inside of chicken with damp paper towels. Place chicken in a roasting pan. Tuck wing tips under breast.

Break bread into small pieces and put in a medium-size mixing bowl. Add onion, basil, and ⅓ cup of broth. Mix together well and fill body cavity of chicken with mixture. Put leftover broth in refrigerator.

Rub chicken with butter and sprinkle with seasoning salt. Carefully set roasting pan in hot oven.

Scrub potatoes under cold water and pat dry. Prick skins several times with a fork. Put a can of cranberry sauce in refrigerator if it is not already there.

4:45—Place potatoes on rack in oven around roasting pan. Be careful not to touch any part of oven.

That does it; you're finished. Let mom or dad do the rest.

6:00—Cook 2 boxes of frozen broccoli according to package directions.

Remove chicken and potatoes to a platter. Skim fat from drippings in pan. Add water to refrigerated broth to make 2 cups. Stir flour into broth until smooth. Add to drippings and cook over medium heat, stirring until gravy thickens. Pour into gravy bowl.

Melt 2 tablespoons of butter in a small saucepan. Stir in 2 tablespoons lemon juice and 1 teaspoon of chopped parsley. Drain broccoli well, place in a serving dish, and pour lemon-butter over it. Take cranberry sauce from refrigerator and empty can into a serving dish.

Serves 6 (or 4 with sandwich fixings for next day).

6:20—*Dinner is served.*

PUNGENT PORK CHOPS
RICE OR NOODLES
CUCUMBER SALAD

PUNGENT PORK CHOPS

- 4 tablespoons vegetable oil
  Flour for dredging
- 4 pork chops, trimmed of fat
- 1 small onion
- 1 green pepper
- 4 stalks celery (discard tops)
- 1 can condensed tomato soup
- 4 tablespoons red wine vinegar
- 2 tablespoons brown sugar
- ¼ teaspoon salt

4:00—Preheat oven to 325° F. Put a Dutch oven on top of the stove over medium heat and add oil. Put some flour on a plate and turn pork chops in it. Put chops in pot and brown on both sides.

While chops are browning, peel and slice onion, and seed and slice green pepper. Chop up celery.

Mix tomato soup, vinegar, brown sugar, and salt in a small bowl.

Remove pork chops from pot and put on a plate. Using pot holders, carefully pour grease into an empty can to dispose of later.

Put chops back into Dutch oven and arrange onions, pepper, and celery over them. Pour soup mixture over everything as evenly as possible. Cover pot and put in oven.

That does it; you're finished. Let mom or dad do the rest.

6:00—Test chops for doneness—a fork should pierce them easily. Start a saucepan of water to boil for rice or noodles. Peel and slice 2 cucumbers and mix with oil, vinegar, salt, and pepper in a glass bowl. Add a little fresh chopped dill or parsley if you have it. Bring Dutch oven, salad, and rice or noodles to the table.

Serves 4.

6:30—*Dinner is served.*

SAFETY RULES

1.   Always turn off the oven, burner, heating unit, or electrical appliance as soon as you are finished with it. Never leave a burner or electrical appliance on when you leave the house.

2.   When using a knife, cut away from your hand. Use a vegetable peeler to peel fruit and vegetables. Never try to open a can with a knife; always use a can opener.

3.   Turn all pot handles away from the edge of the stove so they cannot be bumped.

4.   Pour hot things away from you; the steam coming from them can burn you. Stand back whenever you open the oven—a very hot puff of air will rush out at first.

5.   Use pot holders for lifting hot pots and pans. Equipment that has been used on the stove or in the oven will stay too hot to touch for quite a while.

6.   Don't touch electrical cords or appliances when your hands are wet.

7.   Wipe up spills immediately. It's easier to clean them right away, and they could cause falls if left on the floor.

8.   If grease in a skillet or broiler pan catches fire, do not put water on it. Instead, smother fire with a lid or by pouring baking soda or salt on it.

9.   Do not open canned foods if the cans appear bulged or are leaking. Do not use canned food if it is unusually cloudy or smells unusual.

10. Parents: Store cleaning supplies, medicines, insecticides, and other household chemicals away from cooking utensils and ingredients. Keep sharp knives in a separate drawer away from other utensils, and warn children specifically about everything they should not touch.

KITCHEN TIPS

Get Ready

1.   Tie back long hair, roll up long sleeves and, if you like, put on an apron to keep your clothing clean.

2.   Wash your hands with soap and water.

3. If you have a double sink or a sink large enough that it won't be in your way, get out a dishpan and fill it with soapy water.

Get Set

1. Get out all of the ingredients, equipment, and recipes you will be using.

2. If you will be using the oven, set it to the temperature listed in the recipe. This will give it time to preheat (warm up). Get out pot holders.

3. If your recipe calls for greasing a pan, lightly rub the sides and bottom with shortening.

Go

1. Measure ingredients using standard measuring spoons and cups. Use metal or plastic cups for dry ingredients, and glass or clear plastic cups for liquids.

2. Fill dry measures a little above the top, then run the straight edge of a spatula across the surface to make the top even with the top of the spoon or cup. Catch the extra on waxed paper or paper towel. Use the level amount. Return the extra to the container.

3. Set liquid measuring cups on a level surface. Look at the cup so that the line you are going to use is at eye level. Fill until liquid reaches that line.

4. Butter may be measured by cutting it at the lines marked on the stick. Shortening should be pressed into a measuring cup and made level.

5. If your recipe calls for eggs, wash them, crack one into a cup, then add to your mixture. Repeat with the rest of the eggs so that if one is spoiled you can discard it without ruining the rest or the other ingredients.

6. As soon as you are finished with an ingredient, return the container to its place or discard it if empty. Throw away egg shells, peelings, and other trash as soon as you have finished with them. Rinse the equipment as you use it and place it in the soapy water.

BAKE-ALONG-WITH-DINNER DESSERT COLLECTION

Here are some delicious family desserts that may be substituted for the desserts in the menus. All can be baked at the same time as the main dish you are making.

JAM SANDWICH PUDDING

> 1 teaspoon butter
> ½ cup strawberry, raspberry, cherry, or apricot jam or preserves
> 8 slices white bread
> 3 eggs
> 3 cups milk
> 3 tablespoons sugar
> ½ teaspoon vanilla
>   Cinnamon sugar (optional)

Preheat oven to 375° F.

Butter a 12-by-8-by-2-inch baking dish.

Divide preserves onto 4 slices of bread; spread to cover bread. Top each with another bread slice. Using a table knife, cut each sandwich into two triangles. Arrange in baking dish.

Beat eggs in a medium bowl using rotary beater or wire whisk. Beat in milk, sugar, and vanilla. Pour over sandwiches, making sure all bread is moistened. Sprinkle with cinnamon sugar, if desired.

Set baking dish in a shallow pan containing ½ inch of warm water. Place in oven. Bake for 40 minutes, or until a table knife inserted in center comes out clean.

Makes 6–8 servings.

SCANDINAVIAN APPLESAUCE TORTE

⅓ cup butter
1½ cups graham cracker crumbs
1 teaspoon cinnamon
1 jar (1-lb 8-oz size) applesauce
1 pint vanilla, coffee, or butter pecan ice cream (optional)

Preheat oven to 375° F.

Melt butter in a small saucepan over low heat. Stir in graham cracker crumbs and cinnamon.

Grease an 8-inch-round baking dish. Make a layer using one-fourth of crumbs. Add one-third of applesauce. Continue layering until all applesauce and crumbs are used. End with a layer of crumbs.

Bake for 20 minutes. Using pot holders, remove from oven and place on wire rack to cool slightly.

To serve, loosen edges and invert onto serving plate. Cut into wedges and serve with ice cream, if desired.

Makes 6 servings.

CHOCOLATE SNACK CAKE

¼ cup oil
2 squares (2-ozs) unsweetened baking chocolate
⅔ cup sugar
2 cups biscuit mix
2 eggs
1 teaspoon vanilla
½ cup milk
¼ cup chopped walnuts, pecans, or peanuts

Preheat oven to 375° F.

Grease an 8-by-8-by-2-inch baking pan.

In a medium saucepan, warm oil and chocolate until chocolate is completely melted. Set off heat until slightly cooled—5–8 minutes.

Add sugar, biscuit mix, eggs, vanilla, and milk to mixture in a saucepan. Stir together until well combined. Turn into prepared baking pan. Sprinkle with nuts and bake for 25 minutes, or until surface springs back when gently pressed with fingertip.

Makes 6 servings.

Tip:

To substitute cocoa for baking chocolate: Use 3 level tablespoons of cocoa and 1 tablespoon of oil or shortening for each 1-ounce square of baking chocolate.

CREAMY LEMON PIE

      One 9-inch frozen pie shell
- 2 eggs
- ¾ cup granulated sugar
- 2 tablespoons flour
- 2 tablespoons cornstarch
- ¼ teaspoon salt
- 1 tablespoon oil
- ½ cup lemon juice

      Whipped cream or whipped topping (optional)

Preheat oven to 375° F.

Remove pie shell from freezer. Set in a warm place to thaw slightly.

In a medium bowl, beat eggs with a wire whisk or rotary beater until well combined and frothy. Add sugar, flour, cornstarch, salt, and oil. Beat until well combined. Stir in lemon juice and ½ cup of water until well mixed.

Set pie shell on a small cookie sheet or pizza pan. Pour lemon mixture into shell. Carefully place in oven (be sure to use a pot holder) and bake for 30 minutes, or until filling appears firm and crust is golden.

Let cool at least 30 minutes before serving. Longer cooling is even better. Serve with whipped cream or whipped topping, if desired.

Makes 4–6 servings.

CHAPTER THREE
MOSTLY MEATLESS MEALS

Deciding what to make for dinner, particularly on weekdays when time is of the essence, grows more difficult from day to day. For variety (also for health, according to nutritionists), the once-a-week meatless dinner can be a delicious alternative to the meat entrees that most of us rely on. This section offers suggestions for meatless meals that are simple to make and reasonably painless on the pocketbook.

GARDEN VEGETABLES WITH CHEDDAR CHEESE
DILL BREAD
LEMON SHERBET OR FRUIT SALAD WITH COCONUT
LEMONADE OR WHITE WINE

This skillet dinner is a treasury of fresh garden vegetables. Mixed with rice, in a tangy, light tomato sauce, and topped with bubbly melted cheese, the vegetables make a meal hearty enough for the hungriest member of your family. No accompaniments are really necessary, but if you like, add a crunchy loaf of French bread spread with a blend of butter, garlic, and dill, and then warmed. For dessert, two cool and light choices are lemon sherbet and fresh fruit salad sprinkled with coconut.

GARDEN VEGETABLES WITH CHEDDAR CHEESE

    2 small cloves garlic, minced
    2 tablespoons vegetable oil
    1 medium onion, chopped
    1 large red pepper, chopped
    1 large green pepper, chopped
    2 small zucchini, sliced
    2 small summer squash, sliced
    ½ cup fresh peas
    1 stalk broccoli, chopped
    ½ lb spinach, chopped
    6 large mushrooms, sliced
    2 large tomatoes, chopped
    2 tablespoons Worcestershire sauce
    2 tablespoons soy sauce
    1 can (6-oz size) tomato paste (optional)
    2 tablespoons sour cream
 1⅓ cups quick-cooking rice
    Salt and pepper to taste
    2 cups grated sharp cheddar cheese

In a very large skillet over medium heat, sauté garlic in oil until golden. Add onion and red and green pepper pieces. Cook until onions are translucent.

Stir in zucchini, squash, peas, broccoli, and spinach. Cook, stirring frequently, for 5 minutes. Add mushrooms and tomatoes. Cook, stirring, until mushrooms are wilted.

Stir in Worcestershire sauce, soy sauce, tomato paste, sour cream, rice, salt, and pepper. Stir all ingredients until well mixed. Cover and cook for 10 minutes, or until rice is done.

Sprinkle cheese evenly over top. Cover skillet and heat for 3 minutes more, or until cheese is melted. Cut into wedges and serve.

Serves 4.

VEGETABLE CURRY
CUCUMBERS AND YOGURT
RICE OR BAKED POTATOES
CHUTNEY
WHOLE WHEAT PITA

There are no firm rules about which vegetables to use in this curry. Use whatever looks fresh, what your family likes, and your favorite seasonal specialties.

To round out this meal for 4–6, serve chutney and rice or baked potatoes, and some whole wheat pita.

VEGETABLE CURRY

¼ cup vegetable oil
1 medium onion, sliced
2 cloves garlic, crushed
2–3 tablespoons curry powder, or to taste
Pinch of red pepper flakes
1 small cauliflower, broken into florets
2 carrots, scraped and chopped
¼ lb green beans, trimmed
1½ cups water
1½ tablespoons tomato paste
Salt and pepper to taste
1 small head broccoli, chopped
Juice of ½ lemon

Add oil, onion, and garlic to a large skillet or wok. Stir over medium heat until onions are softened. Add curry powder and pepper flakes and continue stirring 1–2 minutes more.

Add remaining ingredients except broccoli and lemon juice, and bring to a boil. Cover tightly, lower heat, and simmer gently until vegetables are nearly tender, 12–15 minutes. Add broccoli and continue cooking 5–7 minutes more, or until done to desired tenderness.

Remove pot from heat, add lemon juice, and adjust seasonings.

CUCUMBERS AND YOGURT

> 3–4 cucumbers, peeled and thinly sliced
>   1 tablespoon coarse or kosher salt
>   1 cup plain yogurt
>   Lemon juice to taste

Combine cucumbers and salt in a bowl. Allow to stand about 30 minutes. (You may be tempted to eliminate this step. Don't, unless you want to have a bitter taste in your mouth long after dinner!)

Rinse cucumbers well in cold water and squeeze dry in a clean cloth, extracting as much water as you can. Combine cucumbers with yogurt. Add lemon juice to taste.

ASPARAGUS AND EGGS I OR ASPARAGUS AND EGGS II
GARLIC BREAD

ASPARAGUS AND EGGS I

> 1½ pounds fresh asparagus
>   4 tablespoons butter or oil
>   ½ cup chicken broth
>   ½ cup grated Parmesan cheese
>   6 eggs

Wash asparagus and snap off tough ends; with a carrot scraper, scrape off large scales.

Cut stalks diagonally into 2-inch pieces. If bottom pieces are thick, split them. Heat butter in a skillet that has a cover. Sauté asparagus, stirring to coat with oil, for 2–3 minutes. Add chicken broth and cheese, stir for a minute or two, and cover. Let simmer for about 5 minutes, stirring occasionally until mixture thickens and asparagus is just fork-tender.

Slide 6 eggs into mixture and cover. Simmer until eggs are set.
Makes 3 servings.

ASPARAGUS AND EGGS II

1½ pounds fresh asparagus
6 eggs
   Melted butter
   Grated Parmesan cheese

Wash asparagus and snap off tough ends; with a carrot scraper, scrape off large scales.

Drop asparagus into boiling salted water and cook until just tender when tested with a fork, about 5–10 minutes, depending on size.

Meanwhile, have water boiling for poached eggs; have eggs ready to be slipped into the pan.

When asparagus is done, drain carefully and well, and keep warm while poaching eggs.

To serve, place each serving of asparagus on the dinner plate, top with 2 poached eggs, pour on some melted butter, and add a liberal sprinkling of Parmesan cheese. Or put all asparagus in a buttered baking dish, put all 6 poached eggs on top, pour melted butter over all, and sprinkle with Parmesan cheese. Put dish in a hot oven for 2–3 minutes.

Makes 3 servings.

GARLIC BREAD

There are many ways to make garlic bread, and you can, of course, do it as you like. A traditional Italian way is to slice a loaf of Italian bread, toast the slices in the oven, rub one side of each hot slice with garlic, and brush with olive oil. Another way is to soften some butter, add mashed garlic and parsley or Italian herb seasoning, and spread the herbed butter on a loaf of Italian bread that has been sliced not quite all the way through. Wrap it all in aluminum foil and warm in the oven while you're doing everything else.

SPAGHETTI PRIMAVERA
ROMAINE AND WATERCRESS SALAD WITH VINAIGRETTE
ITALIAN BREAD

Here is a recipe for Spaghetti Primavera (spaghetti with vegetable sauce) that takes advantage of the tender, young green peas that appear in the spring.

To round out the meal, you might want to make a salad of romaine and watercress with vinaigrette (5 parts salad oil, 1 part white wine vinegar, a liberal dab of Dijon mustard, salt, and pepper), some crunchy Italian bread and, if you like, a fruit compote for dessert.

SPAGHETTI PRIMAVERA

1	lb thin spaghetti
2	tablespoons butter
4	tablespoons olive oil
4	garlic cloves, finely chopped
1	cup chopped scallions
½	cup chopped celery
1	cup shelled fresh or 1 package frozen peas
1	cup diced zucchini
½	cup chopped parsley
1	cup sliced mushrooms
6–12	cherry tomatoes, cut in half
½	cup heavy cream
	Dash of dry vermouth (optional)
	Dash of lemon juice (optional)
4–5	fresh basil leaves, chopped (optional)
½	teaspoon dried oregano
	Dash of nutmeg or mace (optional)
	Salt and freshly ground black pepper
	Parmesan cheese (garnish)

Preheat oven to 350° F. Put an ovenproof platter in to warm.

Put a large pot of water over high heat for spaghetti, which should be cooked according to instructions on package. (Aim at adding pasta to boiling water about the same time as you are adding parsley, mushrooms, and tomatoes to skillet.)

Heat butter and oil in a large skillet. Add garlic, scallions, celery, peas, and zucchini. Simmer around 3–4 minutes.

Add parsley, mushrooms, and tomatoes, and cook 4 minutes more.

Add cream, dry vermouth, lemon juice, and seasonings. Simmer 3–4 minutes, but do not bring sauce to a boil.

At this point, test spaghetti. If it is done, drain and return to pot. Mix sauce together with spaghetti; turn out onto heated platter. Eat immediately with Parmesan cheese.

Serves 4–5.

**BAKED NOODLES FLORENTINE
TOMATO AND ROMAINE SALAD WITH
OIL AND VINEGAR DRESSING
WARM ONION ROLLS
FRESH FRUIT AND COOKIES**

Our recipe for Baked Noodles Florentine costs about 55 cents a serving—and you won't be shortchanging your family nutritionally since the milk, eggs, and cheese provide lots of protein. We hope you and your family will like the change.

BAKED NOODLES FLORENTINE

     1 package (8-oz size) extra-broad noodles
        Salt
     1 container (16-oz size) creamed cottage cheese
     2 tablespoons Parmesan cheese
     1 teaspoon basil
     2 eggs
  1½ cups milk
     2 packages (10-oz size) frozen chopped spinach
     ¼ lb natural cheddar cheese

In a large saucepan, cook noodles in 3 quarts of boiling salted water according to package directions. Drain.

Butter a shallow, 2-quart, refrigerator-to-oven-type baking dish. Mix together noodles, cottage cheese, Parmesan cheese, ½ teaspoon of salt, and ½ teaspoon of basil.*

Preheat oven to 375° F. Beat eggs slightly; add milk and ½ teaspoon of salt. Pour over noodle mixture and bake for 30 minutes.

Meanwhile, cook spinach according to package directions, adding salt and ½ teaspoon of basil. Drain well.

Spread spinach over top of casserole. Slice cheddar cheese into julienne strips and arrange diagonally over spinach. Return to oven. Bake until custard is set and cheese is melted—about 10–15 minutes.

Makes 6 servings.

---

*Note: Casserole may be prepared to this point the night before, covered tightly, and refrigerated.

SALADE NIÇOISE
VINAIGRETTE DRESSING
ITALIAN OR FRENCH BREAD
COOL, CREAMY FRUIT SOUP

Here is a recipe for a salad so full of good things to eat that all you will need to round out the meal is some good, crunchy French or Italian bread, milk or fruit juice for the children, white wine or iced tea for the grownups, and a dessert (ice cream and cookies, or the Cool, Creamy Fruit Soup).

Don't feel you must follow this recipe to the last detail. If you're pressed for time, you can use canned potatoes and canned whole green beans. And anything but the tuna can be left out, although it would be a shame to omit the beans or potatoes!

SALADE NIÇOISE

  2 medium potatoes, boiled, peeled and sliced as for potato salad
  ½ lb green beans, cooked until tender, but not soft
  2 hard-boiled eggs, peeled and sliced
  ½ sweet red onion, paper thinly sliced
  1 large can (or 2 medium cans) tuna, drained and broken into chunks
  ½ cup canned pitted black olives, drained, or 1 cup Mediterranean-style black olives sold in bulk at delicatessens
  ½ green pepper, sliced into thin rounds
  3–4 small tomatoes, cored and quartered
  6–8 canned anchovy fillets, drained
  1 head Boston lettuce or ½ head romaine, pulled apart
  ½ cup diced celery

Once you've cooked the potatoes, beans, and eggs, and prepared the rest of the ingredients, making this salad is just a matter of assembly.

In a large salad bowl, toss lettuce leaves with about one-third of Vinaigrette Dressing. Spread leaves around so they cover bottom and sides of bowl.

In another bowl, mix potatoes, celery, and green beans with another one-third of vinaigrette.

Put potato mixture on lettuce leaves and arrange remainder of ingredients on it in any way that seems attractive. Pour remaining vinaigrette over everything.

Serves 4–6.

VINAIGRETTE DRESSING

- ¼ cup white wine vinegar
- 2 tablespoons Dijon mustard
- ½ cup olive oil
- ½ cup salad oil
- 2 tablespoons chopped fresh parsley
- 3 tablespoons chopped fresh basil
  Salt and freshly ground pepper to taste

Put vinegar and mustard in a jar, cover tightly, and shake until mustard is well blended with vinegar. Add remaining ingredients, cover tightly, and shake well again. Taste dressing to make sure it is as tart as you like. If it isn't, add a bit more vinegar.

COOL, CREAMY FRUIT SOUP

- 2 small containers (2 cups) vanilla yogurt
- 2 bananas, sliced
- 1 can pineapple chunks, drained

Combine yogurt, banana slices, and pineapple chunks in a glass bowl and refrigerate until ready to serve.

Serves 4–6.

EGGPLANT AND RICE CASSEROLE
BOSTON LETTUCE AND ENDIVE SALAD
BAKED APPLES OR FRUIT SALAD

This recipe for Eggplant and Rice Casserole, a real stick-to-the-ribs dish, will hearten any family at the end of a winter day.

To round out the meal, add a salad of Boston lettuce and endive with oil and vinegar dressing and baked apples or a fruit salad for dessert.

EGGPLANT AND RICE CASSEROLE

- 1 large eggplant
  Oil as needed
- 2 cups uncooked rice
  Seasoned salt
- 1 large onion
- 1 medium green pepper, diced
- 1 tablespoon fines herbes (or substitute a selection of basil, chives, marjoram, parsley, and tarragon)
  Pepper
- ¾ cup grated or finely chopped mozzarella cheese
- ¾ cup grated cheddar cheese
- 3 large tomatoes, sliced ¼ inch thick

Cut eggplant into ⅓-inch slices (do not peel). Place slices on a layer of paper toweling. Place another layer of toweling on top. Press down, squeezing as much liquid from eggplant as possible without breaking up slices.

Heat about 2 teaspoons of oil in a large skillet and sauté eggplant slices until tender and slightly browned on both sides. Remove from skillet and set aside.

Cook rice according to package directions, substituting seasoned salt for salt called for on package.

Preheat oven to 375° F.

While rice is cooking, sauté onion and green pepper with fines herbes and a good dash of pepper in skillet used for eggplant until onions are translucent and peppers are tender but not mushy.

When rice is done, stir in onion and pepper.

Combine cheeses.

Assemble casserole: In the bottom of an ungreased 3-quart baking dish, arrange half of eggplant slices, a layer of half of rice mixture, a layer of half of tomato slices, and a layer of half of cheese mixture. Repeat, ending with a layer of cheese. Sprinkle with seasoned salt and pepper. Bake for 15 minutes, or until cheese has melted and casserole is hot and bubbly all the way through.

Serves 4–6.

HARVEST STEW
RICE
COLESLAW
LIME SHERBET WITH SEEDLESS GREEN GRAPES

HARVEST STEW

- 2 tablespoons olive or vegetable oil
- 2 tablespoons butter or margarine
- 1 large red or sweet onion, thickly sliced
- 2 cloves garlic, freshly minced
- 3 medium zucchini, cut into ½-inch rounds
- 1 green pepper, seeded and cut into thin strips
- 3 small tomatoes, peeled and quartered
- 1 can (16-oz size) chickpeas, drained

Start cooking some rice according to directions on package. Heat oil and butter in a large skillet over medium heat. Add onion slices and cook for a few minutes. Add garlic, zucchini, and green pepper, and cook until slightly browned. Stir in tomatoes and chickpeas. Cover skillet and turn down heat to low. Simmer slowly for about 25 minutes. During last 10 minutes of cooking, check vegetables for liquid. If stew is soupy, uncover and cook off a little liquid.

Now check rice. If all water has been absorbed, stir in a little butter and transfer rice to a serving bowl. Garnish with paprika and some chopped parsley, if you like. Serve stew over rice.

To make coleslaw, core and shred half a green cabbage and put in a glass bowl. Add equal parts of yogurt and mayonnaise—enough so that cabbage is well coated. Add lemon juice, salt, and pepper to taste.

Serves 4.

Tip:
The easy way to peel a clove of garlic is to whack it with the flat side of a knife, then pull off the skin.

FETTUCCINE CON VERDURE
ROMAINE AND TOMATO SALAD
WHOLE WHEAT ITALIAN BREAD
ORANGE AND GRAPE COMPOTE

Fettuccine con Verdure (noodles with fresh vegetables), a hearty pasta and vegetable combination in a creamy sauce, will cheer your family on a cold evening. To round out the meal, you might add a salad of romaine and thinly sliced tomatoes with your favorite oil and vinegar dressing, a crusty loaf of whole wheat Italian bread, and a compote of mandarin oranges and green grapes for dessert.

FETTUCCINE CON VERDURE

½ lb (½ small head) broccoli
½ lb (½ small head) cauliflower
½ lb green beans
   Salt
¾ lb fresh or dried fettuccine
¼ lb mushrooms
¼ cup (½ stick) butter
½ teaspoon dried basil
½ cup heavy cream
2 tablespoons chopped fresh parsley
½ cup Parmesan cheese
   Freshly ground black pepper to taste

Put 3 quarts of water in a large kettle over high heat to cook fettuccine.

Wash broccoli and cauliflower and break into florets. Wash green beans; trim ends and cut beans in half. Place vegetables in a medium saucepan. Add ½ teaspoon of salt and enough water to cover. Bring water to a boil and cook vegetables 3–5 minutes.

Add fettuccine and 1 tablespoon of salt to boiling water in the large kettle and cook 5–7 minutes for fresh pasta, 10–12 minutes for dried.

Wash and slice mushrooms. Melt 1 tablespoon of butter in a medium saucepan. Sauté mushrooms until golden. Add remaining butter, ½ teaspoon of salt, and basil. When butter has melted, turn off heat and gently stir in cream.

Drain fettuccine and vegetables well. Dry large kettle and add to it fettuccine, vegetables, mushroom sauce, parsley, and ¼ cup of Parmesan cheese. Mix well.

Turn out pasta onto a large warmed serving platter and top with remaining cheese and some freshly ground pepper.

Serves 4–6.

SOUTHERN COMFORT CASSEROLE
VEGETABLE SALAD
CRUSTY ITALIAN BREAD
VANILLA ICE CREAM WITH HEAVENLY HOT FUDGE SAUCE

SOUTHERN COMFORT CASSEROLE

- 1 cup uncooked grits
- ½ cup melted butter
- 6 tablespoons milk
- ½ lb extra-sharp cheddar cheese
- 3 eggs
- 2 cans (4-oz size) whole green chilies, drained and chopped

Preheat oven to 400° F.

Cook grits according to directions on package. Remove from heat and let cool 10 minutes.

Add butter, milk, and cheese, and mix well. Beat in eggs, 1 at a time. Add chilies and gently combine.

Bake in a greased casserole for 1 hour.

Serves 6.

VEGETABLE SALAD

- ½ head Boston lettuce
- 1 zucchini, thinly sliced
- 1 cucumber, thinly sliced
- 2 small tomatoes, quartered
- ½ red onion, thinly sliced
- 5 large mushrooms, thinly sliced
- ½ cup alfalfa sprouts (optional)

Wash and tear lettuce into bite-size pieces. Put all ingredients in a large salad bowl and refrigerate. When ready to eat, toss salad with dressing below.

CREAMY SALAD DRESSING

  ½ cup oil
  3 tablespoons fresh lemon juice
  1 egg
  ¼ teaspoon dry mustard
  ¼ teaspoon sugar
    Salt to taste

Put all ingredients in a blender and run on high speed until well combined.

HEAVENLY HOT FUDGE SAUCE

  2 squares unsweetened chocolate
  ⅓ stick butter
  ½ cup sugar
  ¼ cup heavy cream
  ½ teaspoon vanilla

Put all ingredients except vanilla in a small, heavy saucepan over medium-low heat. Beat constantly with a wooden spoon and bring to a slow boil. Turn off heat and stir in vanilla. Let sauce stand in warm place until ready to serve.

CREAMY MACARONI-AND-CHEESE CASSEROLE
VEGETABLE SALAD
ITALIAN BREAD
SLICED ORANGES
CHOCOLATE CHIP COOKIES

Crunchy on top and creamy beneath, this tasty baked pasta dish is golden with cheddar cheese. For a fun variation, mix elbow macaroni with another shape of pasta, such as shells or bows. If there are any leftovers (which is unlikely!), the casserole makes a tasty hot or cold lunch. For a healthful and satisfying meatless dinner, serve with a crisp and colorful salad of fresh vegetables.

CREAMY MACARONI-AND-CHEESE CASSEROLE

- ¾ lb uncooked elbow macaroni (about 6 cups cooked)
- 2 eggs, lightly beaten
- ½ cup milk
- 1 can (11-oz size) cheddar cheese soup
- ½ teaspoon black pepper
- ½ teaspoon salt
- 3 cups grated cheddar cheese
- ¼ cup bread crumbs

Preheat oven to 350° F.

Cook macaroni according to directions on package. Drain cooked pasta and set aside.

In a deep, ovenproof casserole dish, combine eggs, milk, cheddar cheese soup, pepper, and salt until blended. Mix in pasta until well coated. Add 2½ cups of cheese and stir. Sprinkle remaining cheese on top. Sprinkle bread crumbs over all.

Bake for 30 minutes, or until top is golden.

Serves 4.

VEGETABLE SALAD

- 2 large tomatoes, sliced
- 1 cucumber, thinly sliced
- 1 green pepper, sliced
- 5 strips sweet pimiento, diced
- 2 tablespoons chopped red onion

Combine all ingredients in a salad bowl and refrigerate. When ready to serve, toss salad with this dressing:

- 2 tablespoons olive oil
- 2 tablespoons red wine vinegar
- 3 hard-boiled egg yolks, mashed
  Salt and pepper to taste

Put all ingredients in a bowl and mix with a fork until well combined.

SPANISH RICE
CUCUMBER AND AVOCADO SALAD
CANNED PLUMS WITH SOUR CREAM

Hearty rice flavored with tomato and onion and covered with cheese makes a satisfying skillet supper, which goes well with the salad of crunchy cucumber and smooth avocado.

SPANISH RICE

>   2 tablespoons butter
>   2 tablespoons oil
>   4 medium onions, sliced
>   1 clove garlic, finely minced
>   1 green pepper, chopped
>   1 cup uncooked rice
>   1 can (10¾-oz size) condensed chicken broth
>   1 can (6-oz size) tomato paste
>   Dash of pepper
>   2 cups grated cheddar, Muenster, or Monterey Jack cheese

In a large skillet over medium heat, melt butter and add oil. Lower heat and add onions, garlic, and green pepper. Sauté until onions are translucent; do not let onions brown.

Stir in rice, broth, tomato paste, pepper and 1 cup of water. Cover and simmer for 20 minutes, or until rice is tender.

Sprinkle cheese over rice, cover, and let sit for 2 minutes.

Serves 4.

CUCUMBER AND AVOCADO SALAD

>   2 medium cucumbers
>   1 large ripe avocado
>   1 tablespoon lemon juice
>   3 tablespoons vinegar
>   1 small onion
>   ¼ teaspoon dried dill
>   4 cherry tomatoes

Peel cucumbers and thinly slice into a large bowl. Peel and slice avocado into bowl. Sprinkle with lemon juice and vinegar. Chop onion into bowl, add dill, and toss. Turn salad into 4 small bowls and garnish each serving with a cherry tomato.

TOMATO-PEA SOUP
TUNA AND AVOCADO SALAD
CRUNCHY ITALIAN BREAD
MEXICAN SUNDAES
LEMONADE OR
CHILLED WHITE WINE

Try this lovely light supper for four on one of those sultry evenings when you don't want to linger by the stove!

TOMATO-PEA SOUP

       1 can condensed tomato soup
       1 can condensed green pea soup
       ½ soup can heavy cream
    2–3 tablespoons sherry

Pour contents of both cans of soup into a large saucepan and put on top of the stove over medium heat. Add heavy cream to pot. Add 1½ cans of water to soup and mix very well with a wooden spoon. Bring soup to a simmer and add sherry. Cook another minute or so and divide into 4 soup bowls. Serve at once.

TUNA AND AVOCADO SALAD

       2 large avocados
         Juice of ½ lemon
       1 large can tuna fish, drained
       2 stalks celery, finely chopped
       ½ small sweet onion, finely chopped
       ¼ green pepper, cored and diced
       ½ cup mayonnaise
    ¼–½ cup yogurt
         Pinch of dried thyme
         Salt and pepper to taste
       1 small head Boston lettuce

Cut avocados in half, take out pits, and sprinkle a little lemon juice over each half. Set aside.

Turn tuna into a medium-size bowl. Add remaining ingredients except lettuce and mix well.

Wash and tear lettuce into bite-size pieces. Arrange on 4 plates. Put an avocado half in the center of each bed of lettuce and fill cavity with tuna salad mixture.

Pour over each serving some of following dressing:

MUSTARDY VINAIGRETTE

⅔ cup vegetable oil
⅛–¼ cup red wine vinegar
3 tablespoons Dijon mustard
Salt and pepper to taste

Mix ingredients in a small jar. Cover and shake until creamy and completely combined.

MEXICAN SUNDAES

1 pt vanilla ice cream
⅔ cup prepared chocolate sauce
⅔ cup salted peanuts

Divide ice cream into 4 small glass bowls. Pour some chocolate sauce over each helping. Top each sundae with a liberal sprinkling of peanuts.

SPINACH LINGUINE WITH RED CLAM SAUCE
ENDIVE AND WATERCRESS SALAD
ITALIAN BREAD
CHILLED WHITE WINE, RED WINE, OR CIDER
SEEDLESS GRAPE SURPRISE

SPINACH LINGUINE WITH RED CLAM SAUCE

½ cup butter
½ cup olive oil
3–6 cloves garlic, minced or pressed
Salt
1 teaspoon salad oil
1½ lbs spinach linguine or spaghetti
2 cans (6½-oz size) chopped clams
¼ cup white wine
½ cup chopped and peeled fresh Italian tomatoes or drained canned tomatoes
¼ teaspoon pepper
1 cup chopped parsley
Parmesan cheese (optional)

Bring 6 quarts of water to a boil.
Heat butter and oil in a medium skillet. Add garlic and sauté 5 minutes.

Add 1 tablespoon of salt, salad oil, and linguine to boiling water. Cook over medium heat, stirring occasionally, until desired doneness, 8–10 minutes. Drain well, then return linguine to pot.

Drain clams, reserving juice. Add clam juice, white wine, tomatoes, ½–1 teaspoon of salt, and pepper to skillet and simmer for 5 minutes. Add clams and parsley and simmer 3 minutes more.

Add sauce to linguine. Toss until pasta is well coated. Turn out onto a large heated platter. Sprinkle with Parmesan cheese, if desired.

Makes 6–8 servings.

Tip:
To peel small white onions, fresh tomatoes, peaches, apricots, nectarines, et cetera, plunge them into boiling water for half a minute, then run under cold water. Skin slips right off.

SEEDLESS GRAPE SURPRISE

    2 lbs seedless white grapes
    ½ pt sour cream
    1 cup brown sugar

Wash grapes and drain in a colander. Put sour cream and brown sugar in serving dishes and arrange small clumps of grapes on dessert plates. Pass sour cream and brown sugar so that everyone will have a mound of each in which to dip grapes. This dessert is simple, different, and delicious. Children will think so too!

SPINACH SALAD
SAVORY HOT-POTATO DRESSING
BAKED STUFFED PEASANT BREAD
WATERMELON

SPINACH SALAD

Toss salad with oil and vinegar, or, if you're feeling more ambitious, serve it with Savory Hot-Potato Dressing.

> 1 lb spinach, washed and stems removed
> 1 cup sliced mushrooms
> ½ cup diced Swiss cheese
> 3 hard-boiled eggs, thinly sliced

Make sure spinach is dry. Tear into bite-size pieces and place in a large salad bowl. Add mushrooms, cheese, and eggs, and toss gently.

Toss with oil and vinegar or Savory Hot-Potato Dressing.
Serves 4.

SAVORY HOT-POTATO DRESSING

> 2 medium potatoes, peeled and diced
> 6–8 strips bacon
> 1 cup mushrooms
> 1 teaspoon red wine vinegar
> Salt and pepper to taste

Steam or boil potatoes until tender. Drain off liquid and reserve.

Cook bacon until crisp and drain on paper towels. Pour off and discard half of bacon drippings from pan. Sauté mushrooms in remaining drippings until tender. Leave mushrooms in skillet and set aside.

Crumble bacon into potatoes. Add to mushrooms in skillet, along with vinegar and ¾ cup of reserved potato liquid. Cook over low heat, stirring, until hot. Pour over salad and toss gently. Add salt and pepper. Serve warm.

BAKED STUFFED PEASANT BREAD

1	large loaf French or Italian bread
4	tablespoons olive oil
1	large, very ripe tomato, diced
2	cloves garlic, finely minced
12–16	cherry tomatoes, each sliced into thirds
¼–½	lb feta or mozzarella cheese, thinly sliced
10	black olives, pitted and sliced
4	tablespoons grated Parmesan cheese

Preheat oven to 500° F.

Slice loaf in half lengthwise. Scoop out and discard soft interior, leaving about 1 inch, to make a well in each half loaf.

Drizzle 1 tablespoon of oil over each half. Spoon diced tomato into half loaves and press into bread with back of a large spoon.

Sprinkle each half with garlic. Arrange cherry tomatoes, cheese, and olives on each half. Drizzle remaining oil over each half. Sprinkle with Parmesan cheese.

Place each half on a separate sheet of foil and bring foil up to cover bread. Place both halves in oven for 5 minutes. Turn on broiler. Open foil and place bread under broiler just until cheese and edges are golden brown. Serve hot.

Serves 4.

TOMATO-PEPPER OMELET
CANTALOUPE SALAD
PUMPERNICKEL ROLLS
GINGERSNAPS

TOMATO-PEPPER OMELET

- 1 cup farmer or small-curd cottage cheese
- 3 tablespoons grated Parmesan cheese
- 1 teaspoon salt
- 3 tablespoons butter
- 2 green peppers, seeded and chopped
- 2 medium tomatoes, chopped
- 6 eggs
- 1 tablespoon safflower oil

Combine both cheeses with salt in a mixing bowl.

Melt butter in a medium-size cast-iron skillet. (A cast-iron skillet is preferred because you can run it under the broiler. You can, however, use a regular skillet; just slip the omelet onto a broiler-proof baking dish or pan before broiling top.) Add peppers and sauté over medium heat for about 5 minutes. Add tomatoes and continue cooking 2–3 minutes more. Add vegetables to cheese mixture in mixing bowl. Set skillet aside.

Beat eggs until frothy. Add eggs to cheese mixture and stir to blend.

Add oil to skillet and put over low-medium heat. Pour cheese mixture into skillet. Cook for 5–8 minutes, or until eggs are almost set.

Turn on broiler. Place skillet under broiler briefly, until top is puffy and lightly browned (may take less than a minute). Cut omelet into wedges and serve.

Serves 4.

CANTALOUPE SALAD

- 1 ripe cantaloupe
- ¼ ripe honeydew melon, seeded
- ¼ lb seedless green grapes
- 1 tablespoon fresh lime juice (optional)

Quarter cantaloupe and remove rind and seeds. Cut each piece into thin crescent-shaped slices.

Cut honeydew into 2 pieces and trim off rind. Cut each piece into thin crescent-shape slices.

Arrange cantaloupe and honeydew slices on a cold platter. Sprinkle grapes over all.

If desired, drizzle lime juice over melon and grapes.

Serves 4.

SALMON PASTA SALAD
BUTTERED CORN ON THE COB
WARM SOURDOUGH BREAD
STRAWBERRIES WITH POWDERED SUGAR

SALMON PASTA SALAD

This dish, chock full of good things, is perfect for summer appetites.

- 1 lb pasta shells
- 2 cloves garlic, minced
- 4 whole scallions, chopped
- 1 tablespoon butter
- ⅓ cup chopped green pepper
- 1½ cups fresh or frozen peas, cooked
- 2 cans (6½-oz size) blueback salmon
- 3 tablespoons grated Parmesan cheese

Dressing:
- ½ cup olive oil
- 1 tablespoon red wine vinegar
- 1 tablespoon lemon juice
- 1 egg yolk
  Salt to taste
- ¼ teaspoon pepper

Cook pasta according to package directions. Meanwhile, whisk together ingredients for dressing. Drain pasta thoroughly, immediately transfer to a large bowl, and toss with dressing.

Sauté garlic and scallions in butter for 2–3 minutes.

Toss pasta with garlic, scallions, pepper, peas, and salmon. Sprinkle with Parmesan cheese.

Serves 4.

Tip:
Pasta won't stick together if you add a tablespoon of oil to the cooking water.

STUFFED TOMATOES
STRING BEANS WITH PEARS
ROLLS
POUND CAKE WITH BLUEBERRIES

STUFFED TOMATOES

Tomatoes are the glory of summer. These stuffed ones make for a satisfying supper.

- 6 large tomatoes
- 1 cup cooked rice
- ⅓ cup pine nuts or chopped almonds (optional)
- 1 clove garlic, minced
- 2 tablespoons finely minced parsley
- 3 teaspoons oregano
- 1 teaspoon salt
- 4 tablespoons olive oil
- ½ lb (12 small squares) mozzarella cheese
- 3 tablespoons grated Parmesan cheese

Cut a thin slice from top of each tomato. Scoop out pulp. Set tomato "cups" aside. Chop pulp coarsely and put in a bowl.

Add rice, nuts, garlic, parsley, oregano, salt, and 1 tablespoon of oil to tomato pulp. Mix well.

Preheat oven to 400° F.

Arrange tomato cups close together in a baking dish. Put a square of mozzarella in the bottom of each tomato.

Spoon filling into each tomato until tomato is half full. Put another square of mozzarella in each tomato. Now add remainder of filling so that each tomato is stuffed to top. Sprinkle with Parmesan cheese and drizzle remaining 3 tablespoons of oil over all.

Bake for 25 minutes. Spoon some pan juices over each tomato before serving.

Serves 4.

STRING BEANS WITH PEARS

String beans and pears are a delicious, if unusual, combination.

- 1 lb string beans, washed and trimmed
- 2 small pears
- 2 tablespoons butter

Steam string beans or cook in a little water until just tender. Drain thoroughly.

Peel and chop pears into bite-size pieces.

Place beans in a serving dish. Add butter and pears, and toss gently. Serves 4.

ZUCCHINI-CHEESE CUSTARD
CARROT STICKS
WHOLE WHEAT BREAD
PEACHES IN CREAM

ZUCCHINI-CHEESE CUSTARD

This luscious green-vegetable custard has a fresh garden taste.

2½ cups alfalfa sprouts
½ cup bread crumbs
¾ cup diced cheddar cheese
1 clove garlic, minced
2 eggs
¼ cup milk
4–6 small zucchini, grated
3 tablespoons grated Parmesan cheese

Preheat oven to 350° F.

In a food processor or blender, process sprouts, bread crumbs, cheddar cheese, garlic, eggs, and milk on medium speed just until smooth.

In a bowl, combine zucchini with processed ingredients. Pour into well-greased 8-by-8-inch-square baking pan.

Bake custard for about 20 minutes, until set. Sprinkle on Parmesan cheese and bake for several minutes more, or until cheese is lightly browned.

Serves 4.

GAZPACHO
HOT GARLIC BREAD WITH TUNA
APRICOTS

GAZPACHO

If you like, serve this cold Spanish soup topped with croutons.

3–5 medium-size (1½ lbs) ripe tomatoes, halved, skinned, and seeded
 1 medium green pepper, seeded and halved
 1 small onion, quartered
 1 small cucumber, peeled and cut into 4 chunks
 4 slices day-old bread
 4 tablespoons vinegar
 ½ teaspoon sugar
 1 clove garlic, minced
 1 cup tomato juice
  Salt to taste

Put 4 soup bowls in refrigerator to chill. Put all ingredients in a food processor or blender. Process on high speed until mixture is smooth.
Ladle soup into chilled bowls.
Serves 4.

HOT GARLIC BREAD WITH TUNA

 1 loaf French or Italian bread
  Butter
 1 teaspoon garlic salt
 1 can (7-oz size) tuna in oil, drained slightly
  Grated Parmesan cheese

Preheat oven to 450° F.
Cut bread in half lengthwise. Butter each half well. Sprinkle evenly with garlic salt. Spoon tuna onto each half, distributing evenly. Sprinkle each half with cheese to taste. Set bread on a baking sheet.
Bake for several minutes, or until edges of bread are lightly browned. Slice each half loaf in half.
Serves 4.

TRY THESE NO-FAULT OMELETS

Frittatas are flat Italian omelets that are quick, economical, and easy to prepare. You can add your choice of any number of ingredients to the eggs, and all that's needed in the way of special equipment is a heavy skillet and a plate large enough to ocver it. Here are some wonderful recipes to get you started. After you've tried them and mastered the technique of cooking frittatas, use your imagination and your favorite ingredients to whip up your own scrumptious creations. Serve them with bread, salad, and fruit or cookies for well-balanced, tasty meals.

SWISS CHEESE AND APPLE FRITTATA

    5 large eggs
2½ tablespoons butter or margarine
    1 teaspoon oil
    1 large onion, chopped
    2 medium apples, peeled, cored, and sliced into eighths
    1 cup coarsely grated Swiss cheese
    ¼ teaspoon salt
    ⅛ teaspoon white pepper

In a large mixing bowl, beat eggs with a few drops of water until well blended.

Melt 1 tablespoon of butter with oil in a large, heavy skillet. Add onion and sauté over medium heat until golden brown—about 5 minutes. Add apples to onion and continue to cook for 5 minutes more, or until apples are tender.

Add onion and apples to eggs in bowl and stir. Add cheese, salt, and pepper, and mix well.

Add remaining butter to skillet and heat until foamy. Pour in egg mixture and shake to distribute ingredients evenly. Turn down heat to low. Cook for about 12 minutes.

Loosen edges of frittata with a spatula. Gradually work spatula under entire omelet and shake skillet to make sure frittata is completely detached.

Place a dinner plate over skillet. Hold them together with both hands and flip skillet and plate over. Frittata will fall onto plate. Slide frittata back into skillet—bottom side of omelet is now the top. Cook frittata for 5 minutes more. Loosen again if necessary. Cut into wedges.

Serves 3.

SAUSAGE, PEPPER, AND POTATO FRITTATA

      5 large eggs
      2 tablespoons oil
      ½ lb sweet Italian sausage, casings removed, or cooked ham,
         cut into small cubes
      1 (about ¾ cup) potato, thinly sliced and patted dry
      1 medium onion, thinly sliced
      1 medium green pepper, seeded and chopped
   ¼–½ teaspoon salt
         Black pepper to taste
   1½ tablespoons butter or margarine

In a large mixing bowl, beat eggs with a few drops of water until well blended.

Heat 1 tablespoon of oil in a large, heavy skillet. Add sausage and cook, stirring with a fork to break up meat, until sausage is no longer pink. With a slotted spoon, remove sausage from skillet and add to eggs. (If using ham, sauté for 2 minutes.)

Add remaining oil to skillet and sauté potato slices until lightly golden—about 5 minutes. Add onion and continue to cook for about 4 minutes. When onion starts to turn golden, add green pepper and cook for 1 minute more, shaking and stirring ingredients to cook evenly.

Add sautéed vegetables, salt, and pepper to meat and egg mixture. Blend well.

Remove any burnt particles from skillet. Add butter and heat until foamy. Pour in egg mixture and shake to distribute ingredients evenly. Turn heat down low. Cook for about 10 minutes.

Loosen edges of frittata with a spatula. Gradually work spatula under entire omelet and shake skillet to make sure frittata is completely detached.

Place a dinner plate over skillet. Hold them together with both hands and flip skillet and plate over. Frittata will fall onto plate. Slide frittata back into skillet—bottom side of omelet is now the top. Continue to cook for 4 minutes more. Loosen again if necessary. Cut into wedges.

Serves 3.

BROCCOLI, PASTA, AND PARMESAN FRITTATA

- 5 large eggs
- 2 tablespoons oil
- 1–2 cloves garlic, finely chopped
- 1 package (10-oz size) frozen chopped broccoli
  Black pepper to taste
- 1 cup freshly cooked or leftover pasta (leftover macaroni and cheese works well)
- ½ cup grated Parmesan cheese
- 2 tablespoons butter or margarine

In a large mixing bowl, beat eggs with a few drops water until well blended.

Heat the oil in a large, heavy skillet. Add garlic and sauté for 3 minutes. Thaw and press broccoli very dry in a strainer; add to skillet and sauté for 3 minutes. Remove from heat.

Add pepper, pasta, and grated cheese to eggs in bowl and stir. Add broccoli and garlic, and mix well.

Add butter to skillet and heat until foamy. Pour in egg mixture and shake to distribute ingredients evenly. Turn heat down low. Cook for about 8 minutes.

Loosen edges of frittata with a spatula. Gradually work spatula under entire omelet and shake skillet to make sure frittata is completely detached.

Place a dinner plate over skillet. Hold them together with both hands and flip skillet and plate over. Frittata will fall onto plate. Slide frittata back into skillet—bottom side of omelet is now the top. Continue to cook for 3 minutes more. Loosen again, if necessary. Cut into wedges.

Serves 3.

KIELBASA AND SAUERKRAUT FRITTATA

     5 large eggs
     3 tablespoons butter or margarine
     1 cup sauerkraut, well drained
     ½ lb kielbasa, cut into ⅓-inch slices
       Black pepper to taste
 ¼–½ teaspoon salt

     In a large mixing bowl, beat eggs with a few drops of water until well blended.

Melt 1½ tablespoons of butter in a large, heavy skillet. Add sauerkraut and cook over medium heat for about 5 minutes.

Stir sauerkraut into eggs in bowl. Add kielbasa, pepper, and salt.

Add remaining butter to skillet and heat until foamy. Pour in egg mixture and shake to distribute ingredients evenly. Turn down heat to low. Cook for about 8 minutes.

Loosen edges of frittata with a spatula. Gradually work spatula under entire omelet and shake skillet to make sure frittata is completely detached.

Place a dinner plate over skillet. Hold them together with both hands and flip skillet and plate over. Frittata will fall onto plate. Slide frittata back into skillet—bottom side of omelet is now the top. Continue to cook frittata for 3 minutes more. Loosen again if necessary. Cut into wedges.

Serves 3.

ONION, FETA CHEESE, AND RED PEPPER FRITTATA

    5 large eggs
    3 tablespoons butter or margarine
    ½ cup sliced mushrooms
    ½ cup chopped green onions, tops and all
    1 large red pepper, seeded and sliced
    ½ cup crumbled feta cheese
    1 tablespoon dried dill
      Pinch of cayenne pepper
      Pinch of salt (optional)

In a large mixing bowl, beat eggs with a few drops of water until well blended.

Melt 1½ tablespoons of butter in a large, heavy skillet. Add mushrooms and sauté over medium heat for about 2 minutes. Add onions and red pepper, and continue to cook for 1 minute more.

Add mushroom mixture to eggs in bowl and stir. Add cheese and seasonings, and mix well.

Add remaining butter to skillet and heat until foamy. Pour in egg mixture and shake to distribute ingredients evenly. Turn down heat to low. Cook for about 8 minutes.

Loosen edges of frittata with a spatula. Gradually work spatula under entire omelet and shake skillet to make sure frittata is completely detached.

Place a dinner plate over skillet. Hold them together with both hands and flip skillet and plate over. Frittata will fall onto plate. Slide frittata back into skillet—bottom side of omelet is now the top. Contine to cook frittata for 5 minutes more. Loosen again if necessary. Cut into wedges.

Serves 3.

SOUP AND SALAD—THE COOL COMBINATION

As the weather warms, it's a great time to turn off the stove and take a lighter, cooler, more relaxed look at summer eating. One refreshing solution is a supper of cold soup and a main-dish salad.

Consider the cold soup: With a twirl of your blender or food processor, and as quick as you can say "gazpacho," most of the soups that follow can be stashed away in the fridge until you're ready to enjoy them. (While you're at it, whip up a double or triple batch of one of the base soups, Tangy Tomato Soup or Vegetable Bisque, to which you can add all manner of things to make a variety of wonderful cold soups.)

For the second course, crisp some lettuce, slice a few tomatoes and hard-boiled eggs, open a can of tuna, toss with a soupçon of dressing— et voilà, a main-course salad deluxe! The fun of salads is in the creation. You can go wherever your whim or your leftovers take you. Invent your own combinations of greens, vegetables, herbs, meats, seafood, cheese, croutons, and dressings. With a little ingenuity, you can concoct enough variations so that no two salads of this summer need be the same.

Here follows a colorful collection of frosty soups and hearty, appetite-assuaging salads. For a simple summer dinner, choose one salad and one soup (mixing and matching to follow your imagination and the dictates of your hungry family), add a loaf of bread, some cake, ice cream, or fruit for dessert, and your family is artfully and easily fed.

Soups

TANGY TOMATO SOUP

This simple soup can serve as the base for a variety of exciting cold-soup combinations. The zesty garlic-onion influence may be toned down a little for the children by simmering the soup for a few minutes before you chill it.

        5 medium-size ripe tomatoes
        3 cups tomato juice, chilled
        1 medium onion, peeled and coarsely chopped
    2–3 cloves garlic, peeled
     1½ tablespoons sugar
      ½ teaspoon white pepper
        3 tablespoons mixed fresh marjoram and thyme or 1 tablespoon
          mixed dried marjoram and thyme (optional)

Peel, seed, and coarsely chop tomatoes. Put all ingredients in a blender or food processor.

Puree and chill well before serving.

Serves 6.

VEGETABLE BISQUE

Another base soup, this creamy rich vegetable puree looks as elegant as it tastes. The radish slices provide a pretty garnish, but if you can find nasturtiums or squash flowers, use them instead—they're edible and look beautiful.

- 3 small yellow squash, peeled
- 1 large potato, peeled
- 1 large onion, peeled
- 2 medium carrots, scraped
- ¼ teaspoon curry powder
  Pinch of nutmeg
  Pinch of thyme
  Pinch of saffron
  Salt and white pepper to taste
- 2 cups heavy cream or yogurt (or a combination)
  Milk (optional)
  Sliced radishes (garnish)

Slice squash, potato, onion, and carrots in a soup pot and add seasonings. Cover with water and bring to a boil.

When vegetables are tender, drain and puree in a blender or food processor. Cool to room temperature.

Stir in cream and chill. If soup is too thick, thin with a little cold milk. Garnish with radish slices.

Serves 6.

MEXICAN TORTILLA SOUP

A particularly lively quintet of garnishes transforms the simple tomato base into a south-of-the-border firecracker of a soup.

    1 recipe Tangy Tomato Soup
    ½ teaspoon ground cumin
    ½ teaspoon chili powder
  1½ cups finely chopped scallions
  1½ cups peeled, pitted, and cubed avocado, sprinkled with
       lemon juice to prevent darkening
  1½ cups finely shredded iceberg lettuce
  1½ cups grated cheddar cheese
    3 cups packaged tortilla or corn chips

Mix first 3 ingredients and chill.

Put scallions, avocado, lettuce, and cheese in separate small bowls. Set a bowl of tortilla or corn chips at each place.

Serve bowls of chilled soup and pass garnishes.

Serves 6.

FRESH TOMATO BISQUE

    1 recipe Tangy Tomato Soup
  1½ cups sour cream
  1½ cups plain yogurt
    ¼ cup minced fresh dill or parsley

Whirl tomato soup with sour cream in a blender or food processor until well mixed.

Add yogurt and blend for about 4 seconds. If ingredients are not well integrated, continue mixing by hand. Sprinkle with dill or parsley and serve.

Serves 6.

GOLDEN GAZPACHO

Any number of finely chopped garnishes can enhance Vegetable Bisque. Feel free to experiment with whatever herbs and fresh or cooked vegetables you have in your kitchen, or follow this recipe:

1½ cups finely chopped tomatoes
1½ cups finely chopped scallions
1½ cups finely chopped cucumbers
1½ cups cooked peas, chilled
 1 recipe Vegetable Bisque (omit radishes)
 1 teaspoon minced fresh thyme or ⅓ teaspoon dried thyme
 1 teaspoon minced fresh marjoram or ⅓ teaspoon dried marjoram

Put tomatoes, scallions, cucumbers, and peas in separate small bowls.

Serve bowls of Vegetable Bisque, chilled and sprinkled with herbs. Pass bowls of garnishes.

Serves 6.

JELLIED MADRILENE IN AVOCADO SHELLS

What could be a more delightful prelude to a good old-fashioned chicken salad than this jellied soup in an edible shell?

 3 ripe avocados, peeled and halved
 2 cans (13-oz size) madrilene (red consommé), chilled for 8 hours
 6 teaspoons French dressing
 ¾ cup sour cream
 Peppermint leaves or minced chives

Cut a thin slice from bottoms of avocado halves to level them off.

Spoon jellied madrilene into a bowl and stir.

Arrange avocado halves on small plates. Place 1 teaspoon of French dressing in each cavity and top with madrilene. Garnish each with a dollop of sour cream and a peppermint leaf or a sprinkling of chives. Serve immediately.

Serves 6.

RUSSIAN CHLODNIK

This beet-based cold soup from the Ukraine is a nutritious pick-me-up. The wine-red broth, loaded with ham, fish, potatoes, eggs, and dill, is a satisfying meal in a bowl.

   3 cans (10½-oz size) beef consomme, undiluted
   4 cups shredded cooked beets
   3 cups beet liquid
   ¼ cup lemon juice
   3 tablespoons sugar, or more to taste
   1 teaspoon salt
   1 cup chopped cooked ham
   1 cup flaked cooked fish or 1 can (7-oz size) tuna
   2 cups boiled potatoes
   ½ cup thinly sliced scallions
   6 hard-boiled eggs, quartered
  12 thin slices lemon
   1 cup sour cream
   ½ cup minced fresh dill

In a large bowl or soup pot, combine first 6 ingredients and chill until serving time. Cut potatoes into ½-inch cubes and chill.

When it's time to eat, remove large bowl from refrigerator and stir in ham, fish, potatoes, and scallions.

Ladle soup into bowls. Arrange 4 egg quarters and 2 lemon slices attractively in each bowl. Spoon a dollop of sour cream in center of each and sprinkle with dill. Serve immediately.

Serves 6.

Salads

MIXED-GREEN SUPER SALAD BOWL

Lettuce: For more zip per inch of salad, use at least two varieties of lettuce, including one loose-leafed type such as buttercrunch, romaine, or Bibb.

Other greens: Young, tender leaves of fresh leafy vegetables such as watercress, Swiss chard, kale, collards, and spinach also liven up salads. Young leaves of root vegetables such as beets and turnips are bursting with nutrition and snappy flavor, as are the tasty lettuce substitutes (endive, escarole, and dandelion leaves). Whichever greens you use, choose only the freshest leaves, wash in cold water, soak for 5 minutes in ice water to crisp, and drain thoroughly in a colander or wire salad basket. Finally, pat the leaves with paper towels until completely dry and refrigerate in a plastic bag.

Vegetables: Traditional favorites—cucumbers, tomatoes, green peppers, carrots, scallions and radishes—are wonderful in salads, but don't limit yourself to these. Try thinly slicing those vegetables that are more frequently served cooked—mushrooms, small zucchini and yellow squash, edible pea pods, tiny cauliflower and broccoli florets—and add them to your salad raw. Beets, asparagus, and leeks are wonderful additions too, but they should be cooked first.

Dressing: The most basic dressing of all is a vinaigrette. In a jar, combine 1 part vinegar to 3 or 4 parts oil (according to your taste). Add salt and pepper, cover, and shake well. (See also variation on p. 84.)

Herbs: Be adventurous with fresh herbs, which will add another flavor dimension to your salads and dressings. Try chives, parsley, tarragon, mint, anise, sweet marjoram, and dill.

What else? Delicatessen meats—ham, turkey, salami, tongue—canned fish, hard-boiled eggs, cheese, beans, chickpeas, and even rice add nourishment and interest.

CREAM-CHICKEN SALAD

    1 lb mushrooms, thinly sliced
       Oil
    2 teaspoons lemon juice
    6 cups cubed cooked chicken
    1 cup mayonnaise
       Salt and pepper to taste
    ½ cup unsweetened whipping cream
    ¾ cup finely chopped celery
    ¾ cup finely chopped scallions
    ½ cup diced pimientos
       Buttercrunch lettuce
    3 tomatoes, seeded and cut into eighths
    3 hard-boiled eggs, quartered
    1 tablespoon capers, drained

In a skillet, sauté mushrooms in oil with lemon juice (to prevent mushrooms from darkening). When mushrooms are tender, drain and mix in a large bowl with chicken, mayonnaise, salt, and pepper, and chill well.

Just prior to serving, whip cream and fold into salad with celery, scallions, and pimientos.

Arrange lettuce in a bowl or on a platter, top with chicken salad, surround with tomato slices and egg wedges, and sprinkle with capers.

Serves 6.

CHICKPEA-AND-SAUSAGE SALAD ROMANO

It requires a little last-minute cooking, but this hearty, meat-based salad will satisfy even the most robust appetites.

     12 small brown-and-serve pork sausages
      2 large green peppers, seeded and with pith removed
      2 tablespoons oil
      2 cloves garlic, peeled and minced
    1½ cups chopped sweet onion
      2 small (no more than 1½ inches in diameter) zucchini, sliced
      ½ teaspoon oregano
      1 can (20-oz size) chickpeas, well drained
      1 can (16-oz size) red kidney beans, well drained
      1 can (16-oz size) white kidney beans, well drained
      3 hard-boiled eggs, quartered (garnish)
     12 pimiento-stuffed green olives (garnish)
         Salt and pepper to taste
      1 cup vinaigrette (see p. 103)
         Grated Romano cheese

Cut sausages and peppers into ¼-inch-thick strips. In a large skillet, sauté in oil with garlic, onion, zucchini, and oregano until vegetables are tender but still a little crunchy. Add chickpeas and both kinds of beans, and stir gently over medium heat until warm (not hot).

Heap salad onto a platter and garnish attractively with egg quarters and olives. At the table, toss salad with salt, pepper, and enough dressing to coat nicely. Pass cheese.

Serves 6.

COUNTRY SALAD BOWL

- 1 cup broccoli florets
- 1 cup asparagus tips
- 1 cup pea pods
- 2 qts salad greens
- 2 cups Swiss or Gruyère cheese, cut into thin strips
- 2 green peppers, cut into thin strips
- 1 large sweet onion, sliced
- 24 cherry tomatoes

Plunge broccoli, asparagus tips, and pea pods into boiling water for 1 minute. Quickly run under cold water to cool. Drain well and chill.

Crisp salad greens in ice water; drain and blot dry. Select 6–7 of largest, most attractive leaves and use to line bottom of a large salad bowl. Tear remaining greens into bite-size pieces and place in bowl.

Arrange cooked vegetables attractively over salad greens. Arrange cheese, peppers, onion, and tomatoes over all. Serve cold with a sauce-boat of Mimosa Dressing (recipe follows).

Serves 6.

MIMOSA DRESSING

- 2 hard-boiled egg yolks
- 1 cup yogurt
- 1 cup sour cream
- 1 tablespoon sugar mixed with 1 tablespoon lemon juice
- 1 teaspoon minced chives
  Salt and pepper to taste

Press the yolks through a fine sieve or strainer.

Stir, do not beat, all ingredients together. Refrigerate until time to serve.

Makes over 2 cups.

BAKED ZITI
TRICOLOR SALAD
HOT ITALIAN BREAD
OATMEAL-RAISIN COOKIES

Here is a creamy casserole for lovers of pasta and cheese. The bright and crunchy salad rounds out the meal nicely. If there's any baked ziti left over, freeze and reheat for another meal.

BAKED ZITI

    1 lb ziti, penne, or any other short, tubular pasta
    4 cups prepared tomato sauce
    3 cups béchamel sauce (recipe below)
½–¾ cup grated Parmesan or Romano cheese
    2 tablespoons butter or margarine

Preheat oven to 400° F.

Grease a large casserole dish. Cook pasta al dente according to package directions. It will soften more as it cooks in oven. Drain pasta well and put back into pot.

Add tomato and béchamel sauces and half of cheese to pot. Stir.

Turn pasta into casserole dish. Sprinkle with remaining cheese, dot with butter, and bake for 15–20 minutes, or until bubbly and hot. Allow to settle a few minutes before serving.

Serves 4–6.

BÉCHAMEL SAUCE

    3 cups milk
    3 tablespoons butter or margarine
    3 tablespoons flour
    ½ teaspoon salt
    Pinch of nutmeg

In a saucepan, heat milk to a boil.

In another pan, melt butter over low heat. Add flour, stirring constantly with a wire whisk. Cook for 1½–2 minutes, stirring constantly. Do not allow to become brown—it should have a light golden color.

Add hot milk, a little at a time, stirring constantly with whisk. Add salt and nutmeg. Continue to cook and stir until sauce is thick— about 2 minutes.

TRICOLOR SALAD

- ½ head iceberg lettuce, shredded
- 2 carrots, peeled and thinly sliced
- 1 bag (or bunch) radishes, sliced
- 2 scallions, trimmed and sliced
  Bottled dressing

Arrange lettuce, carrots, radishes, and scallions in layers in a glass bowl.

Just before serving, toss with dressing.

CHAPTER FOUR
FAST FOOD FOR TIMES WHEN SOMEONE IS ON THE RUN

The whole family has to eat supper, but sometimes one member is on the run—there's a club meeting, a ball game, or whatever. Here are suggestions for sending that person off with a quick and satisfying meal.

WELSH RAREBIT

- 1 tablespoon butter
- ½ cup diced cheddar cheese
- ¼ cup milk
- ¼ teaspoon dry mustard
  Salt and pepper to taste
- 1 egg yolk
- 2 slices toast

Melt butter in a small saucepan. Add cheese and continue to cook over low heat. When cheese has melted, stir in milk and mustard. Heat, stirring, for 1 minute more. Add salt and pepper, stir, and remove from heat. Beat in egg yolk. Put slices of toast in a bowl and pour cheese sauce over them. A tall glass of milk or cider completes this meal.

BROILED HAM AND CHEESE SANDWICH

- 1 English muffin, split
- 1 tablespoon butter
- 2 tablespoons sour cream
- 4 canned asparagus spears, halved
- 2 thin slices ham
- 4 tablespoons grated Swiss cheese
  Salt and pepper to taste

Preheat broiler. Toast English muffin halves, butter them, and spread with sour cream. Top each half with 4 asparagus halves and cover with a slice of ham. Sprinkle with cheese, salt, and pepper. Broil for 2 minutes, or just until cheese has melted. Serve piping hot with mustard. The sandwich goes well with a cup of hot chocolate.

SAUSAGES WITH CHEESE

- 2 bratwurst or knockwurst
  Dijon mustard
- 2 tablespoons processed cheddar cheese spread
- 1 tablespoon chopped fresh chives

Preheat broiler. Split sausages lengthwise and spread open slightly. Slide under broiler and cook, turning twice, for 5 minutes. Remove sausages from broiler.

Spread cut surfaces of hot sausages with mustard. Mix cheese spread and chives, and spread over mustard. Put sausages back under broiler for 1–2 minutes, or until cheese is hot and bubbly. Rye toast, carrot sticks, and a tall glass of milk make this a complete meal.

BARBECUED BEEFBURGER

> 2 slices bacon (optional)
> ¼ lb ground round
> ¼ cup catsup
> 1 tablespoon light brown sugar
> 1 tablespoon vinegar
> 1 teaspoon instant onion
> Pinch of garlic powder
> Pinch of chili powder

Cut bacon into ½-inch pieces. Fry bacon in a small skillet until almost crisp. Add ground round and break up with a fork. Cook, stirring, until meat is browned.

Add remaining ingredients and simmer for a few minutes. Split and toast a hamburger roll or English muffin. Spoon beef mixture over both halves. Serve with a glass of milk and a wedge of lettuce doused with Russian dressing.

CHICKEN TACOS

> 1 tablespoon chopped onion
> 1 tablespoon chopped green pepper
> 1 can (5-oz size) chunk-style chicken
> 2 tablespoons taco sauce
> 2 taco shells
> Shredded lettuce
> Grated cheddar cheese

Preheat oven to 400° F.

In a small skillet, sauté onion and pepper in a little oil until soft. Stir in chicken, breaking it up with a fork. Add taco sauce and simmer.

Place taco shells directly on oven rack for 3–5 minutes. When they are warm, fill with chicken mixture and scatter lettuce and cheese over top. Serve with cold beer or cider.

MEXICAN HERO

1½ cups canned chili
1 teaspoon chili powder
1 small loaf French or Italian bread
3 tablespoons chopped sweet onion
3 tablespoons grated cheddar cheese

Mix chili and chili powder in a small saucepan and cook over medium heat until bubbling hot. Slice bread almost in half lengthwise. Arrange chili on bottom half of loaf and top with onion and cheese. Serve this extra-hot hero with a tall, cold glass of milk.

EGG AND PEPPER HERO

2 eggs
1 teaspoon garlic salt
Pepper to taste
1 tablespoon oil, butter, or margarine
2 roasted peppers, canned or bottled
1 small loaf French or Italian bread
Chopped parsley

Break eggs into a blender. Add garlic salt and pepper, and blend on medium speed until well mixed. Heat oil in a small, heavy skillet over medium heat. Pour egg mixture into heated skillet and scramble eggs as you usually do.

Chop peppers. Slice bread almost in half lengthwise. When eggs are done, arrange them on bottom half of loaf, top with peppers, and garnish with parsley. Cold cider or hot tea would complete this simple supper.

MONTE CRISTO SANDWICH

2 slices Swiss cheese
1 slice ham
2 slices white bread
1 slice turkey (optional)
1 egg
¼ cup milk
Butter or vegetable oil for frying

Place cheese and ham on one slice of bread; top with turkey. Cover with other slice of bread. Beat egg with milk and dip sandwich in mixture. Turn to coat all sides. Heat butter in a skillet over medium heat. Fry sandwich, turning once, until crispy and golden brown. This toasty sandwich is delicious spread with a little mustard.

PARSLIED OMELET WITH CREAM CHEESE

   2 eggs
   ¼ cup milk
      Dashes of salt and pepper
   2 tablespoons chopped parsley
   1 tablespoon chopped dill (optional)
      Butter for frying
   3 tablespoons cream cheese

   Beat eggs with milk until frothy. Add salt, pepper, and parsley; stir in dill. Heat butter in a skillet over low heat. Pour eggs into skillet and cook without stirring until almost set. Put cheese in center of omelet. When cheese has melted and eggs are set, fold omelet in half and slide onto a plate. Serve this omelet with sliced tomatoes and buttered toast.

TUNA-AVOCADO MELT

   ½ medium avocado
   1 teaspoon lemon juice
   1 tablespoon chopped onion
      Salt and pepper to taste
   1 small can (3½-oz size) tuna fish
   1 teaspoon mayonnaise
   1 pita pocket
   ¼ cup grated Monterey Jack cheese

   Preheat oven to 350° F.
   Mash avocado with lemon juice, onion, salt, and pepper.
   Mash tuna with mayonnaise. Stuff tuna in pita. Top tuna with avocado mixture and cheese. Wrap sandwich in foil and heat in oven 3–5 minutes, or until cheese melts. A glass of iced tea with a sprig of mint completes this meal.

ONION-CHEESE DOGS

  2 hot dogs
  1 small can (7-oz size) kidney beans
  ¼ cup chopped onion
  2 hot dog buns
  ¼ cup grated cheddar cheese

Preheat oven to 400° F.

In a medium saucepan, heat hot dogs in boiling water. Heat kidney beans with onion in a small saucepan.

When hot dogs are heated through, place in buns and top each with half of bean-onion mixture and half of cheese. Wrap buns loosely in foil and warm in oven for 3–5 minutes, or until cheese is slightly bubbly. Serve with a tall glass of milk and an orange.

BOLOGNA AND PEPPER SANDWICH TO GO

  1 hard roll
  4 slices bologna
    Butter
  ½ jar (7-oz size) roasted peppers
2–3 thin slices red onion
    Mustard (optional)

Slice hard roll in half. Fry bologna in a little butter in a skillet over medium heat until browned on both sides. Spread a layer of peppers on bottom half of roll. Add onion slices, bologna, and mustard. Cover with other half of roll. This sandwich is terrific with a sliced kosher dill pickle and a glass of cold milk or a spritzer made with ice, apple juice, and soda water.

CHEESY EGGS IN A RUSH

  1 slice Swiss cheese, diced
  2 eggs, beaten
    Salt and pepper to taste
    Butter
  ½ can (8-oz size) tomato sauce
  1 English muffin

Mix together cheese, eggs, salt, and pepper, and scramble in a little butter in a skillet over medium heat. Heat tomato sauce in a small saucepan. Split, toast, and butter English muffin and put on a plate.

When eggs are done, divide them over muffin halves and top with piping-hot tomato sauce. Orange juice or ice-cold beer is a great accompaniment to this small feast.

TUNA POTATO SANDWICH

    1 tablespoon butter
       Dashes of salt and pepper
       Dash of dried thyme
    2 new potatoes, scrubbed and sliced
    ½ can (7-oz size) tuna, drained
    2 slices pumpernickel bread
    2 tomato slices

Heat butter in a small frying pan over low heat. Stir in salt, pepper, and thyme. Add potatoes and cook, stirring occasionally, until potatoes are done but not mushy—about 5 minutes. Stir in tuna. Cook 2 minutes more. Meanwhile, butter bread. Pile tuna-potato mixture on one slice of bread; top with tomato slices. Cover with other slice of bread.

DEVILISH BAKED EGGS WITH HAM

    2 thin slices ham, cut into strips
    ⅓ cup prepared tomato sauce
       Dash of salt
       Dash of cayenne pepper
    1 teaspoon finely chopped parsley
    2 eggs
    2 slices rye or whole wheat bread
       Butter

Preheat oven to 325° F.

Lightly grease 2 ramekins (or 2 sections of a muffin tin). Arrange ham strips in ramekins. Pour tomato sauce into a bowl; stir in salt, pepper, and parsley. Pour sauce over ham strips. Carefully crack an egg into each ramekin. Bake for about 10 minutes, or until eggs are set. Meanwhile, toast and butter bread. When eggs are done, turn mixture out onto toast.

FRIED MOZZARELLA

    1 egg
    ½ cup seasoned bread crumbs
    4 tablespoons vegetable oil
    ½ lb Mozzarella cheese, sliced into ⅓-inch-thick pieces

Crack egg into a shallow dish, add 2 tablespoons of water, and beat well. Pour seasoned bread crumbs onto a plate. Heat oil in a heavy skillet. Dip cheese slices into egg and then into bread crumbs, coating well. Fry slices in hot oil, turning once, so both sides are nicely browned.

A tossed green salad complements this delicious dish beautifully. Serves 2.

TURKEY DREAM

    3 tablespoons cream cheese
    1 teaspoon Dijon mustard
    1 English muffln, split
    2 strips bacon, cooked and crumbled (optional)
    2 slices turkey or ham
    1 tomato, sliced

Blend cream cheese and mustard thoroughly in a small dish. Toast English muffin halves. Spread with cheese mixture and sprinkle with bacon. Add turkey slices and top with tomato slices.

Serve open-face sandwich with celery sticks and a glass of milk.

BEEF IN A POCKET

      Oil
    ¼ lb ground beef
    1 small onion, sliced
    ⅛ teaspoon salt
      Dash of pepper
    1 whole wheat pita
    1 small tomato, chopped
    ¼ cup crumbled feta cheese

Coat bottom of a small skillet with oil. Add beef, onion, salt, and pepper. Brown meat, breaking it up with a fork. While meat is cooking, warm pita in oven. When meat is ready, drain off fat and spoon meat and onion into pita; add tomato and cheese.

Orange juice or ice-cold beer would be a great accompaniment.

HAM PATTIES

    1 egg
    1 can (6¾-oz size) chunk-style ham
    1 teaspoon instant minced onion
    ¼ cup bread crumbs
       Oil
       Hero roll
       Tartar sauce

In a small bowl, beat egg. Add ham, breaking it up with a fork. Add onion and bread crumbs, and mix thoroughly. Shape into 2 patties.

Pour enough oil into a small skillet to just cover bottom of pan. Cook patties over medium heat, turning to brown on both sides.

Split and toast roll, and spread with tartar sauce. Transfer patties to roll.

Serve with lemonade or beer.

EASY CHICKEN NEWBURG

    1 can (5-oz size) chunk chicken
    1 can (10¾-oz size) cream of mushroom or cream of chicken soup
    4 tablespoons milk
    2 scallions, chopped
       Salt and pepper to taste
    2 slices bread

Combine chicken, soup, and milk in a small saucepan. Heat just to a boil, stirring to blend. Add scallions, salt, and pepper, and simmer for 2 minutes. Toast bread and put on a plate. Spoon chicken mixture over toast.

Serve with carrot or celery sticks and a glass of milk.

CURRIED TUNA MELT

    1 slice rye bread
    1 can (3½-oz size) tuna, drained
    1 small stalk celery, diced
    1 tablespoon chopped walnuts (optional)
    1 tablespoon raisins (optional)
    2 tablespoons mayonnaise
    ¼ teaspoon curry powder
    1 slice Swiss cheese

Toast bread. In a small bowl, flake tuna gently with a fork. Add celery, walnuts, and raisins. Mix in mayonnaise and curry powder. Pile tuna mixture on toast and cover with cheese slice. Run sandwich under broiler briefly to melt cheese.

This savory sandwich goes nicely with a glass of cold apple cider or lemonade.

BACON AND AVOCADO SANDWICH

    4 slices bacon
    ½ avocado, peeled and pitted
    1 teaspoon lemon juice
    1 teaspoon Worcestershire sauce
      Salt and pepper to taste
    2 slices whole wheat bread

Cook bacon until crisp and drain on paper towels. Mash avocado with lemon juice, Worcestershire sauce, salt, and pepper. Toast bread. Spoon avocado mixture onto one slice of toast, top with bacon slices and other piece of toast.

Serve with orange juice.

TUNA PUFF

    3 tablespoons cream cheese
    1 egg yolk
    ½ teaspoon baking powder
      Dash of salt
    1 can (3½-oz size) tuna, drained
    2 slices rye bread

Preheat oven to 400° F.

Combine cream cheese and egg yolk in a small bowl. Beat until smooth. Blend in baking powder and salt. Break up tuna and stir in.

Toast bread lightly. Spread toast with tuna mixture, set on a piece of aluminum foil, and bake for 5–6 minutes, until puffed and browned.

Serve with an apple and tea or cocoa.

FRUITY OMELET

> 1 small apple
> ⅔ cup pitted prunes
> ¼ cup orange or apple juice
> 1 tablespoon butter or margarine
> 2 eggs, beaten with ¼ cup milk
>   Plain yogurt or sour cream

Slice apple into a small bowl. Halve prunes and add to apples with orange or apple juice.

Melt butter in a frying pan. Add fruit mixture and sauté for 3–4 minutes until apple is softened. Pour eggs into pan and stir to combine with fruit mixture.

Cook omelet over low-to-medium heat until set. Slide omelet onto a plate.

Serve with a large dollop of plain yogurt or sour cream, a toasted English muffin, and a tall glass of milk.

CHICKEN RAREBIT

> ½ tablespoon butter
> 4 slices (1-oz size) American cheese
> ½ cup milk
> 1 can (5-oz size) chunk-style chicken
> 1 teaspoon instant minced onion
>   Salt and pepper to taste
> 1 English muffin
> 2 tomato slices

Melt butter in a small saucepan over low heat. Add cheese slices and stir until melted. Slowly stir in milk.

Break up chicken and stir in with onion, salt, and pepper.

Split and toast muffin. Put a tomato slice on each half and divide hot chicken mixture between 2 halves.

A glass of beer or apple juice and a dill pickle round out this meal nicely.

STUFFED PITA

  3 slices bologna
½ green pepper
  1 small onion
  1 tablespoon vegetable oil
  1 tablespoon Dijon mustard
  1 pita

Cut bologna into strips. Slice green pepper and onion.

Heat oil in a frying pan. Sauté pepper and onion until slightly softened but still crunchy. Stir in bologna and mustard. Cover and simmer for 2 minutes.

Meanwhile, warm pita. Spoon bologna mixture into pita.

Serve with carrot sticks and hot tea.

AND WHEN THE ENTIRE FAMILY
IS ON THE RUN . . .

TASTY BEEF TOAST

  2 eggs
  1 lb ground round
½ onion, finely chopped
½ cup seasoned bread crumbs
    Salt and pepper
    Butter or oil
  1 cup sour cream
    Toast

Break eggs into a medium-size bowl and beat with a fork. Add meat, onion, and bread crumbs; add salt and pepper to taste. Mix together. Divide into 4 equal parts and form into patties.

Put a little butter in a skillet on top of stove over medium heat. When pan is hot, add patties. Brown them for about 5 minutes on each side, or until done as your family likes.

Remove patties to a plate. Turn down heat. Add sour cream to pan and mix with drippings. Simmer—but be careful not to boil—until sour cream is warm. Return patties to pan and keep warm over low heat while you make toast.

To serve, put each patty on a piece of toast and pour some sour cream sauce over them.

Serves 4.

You can round out the meal with additional pieces of buttered toast and this easy-to-prepare salad:

EASY ICEBERG CRISP

1 small head iceberg lettuce
1 cup bottled dressing

Put lettuce on your cutting board and quarter it. Pare off core. Slip each section onto a small plate and pour a little dressing over it.

Serves 4.

CHEESY CHICKEN

Butter or oil
2 boned, skinless chicken breasts, cut in half to make 4 pieces
Salt and pepper
4 slices Fontina or Swiss cheese

Preheat broiler. Put a little butter in a large, ovenproof skillet on top of stove over medium heat. While pan is warming, put chicken on a long sheet of waxed paper and cover with another sheet. Flatten each breast by hitting it with bottom of a heavy pot or with a rolling pin.

Sauté chicken in hot butter as quickly as possible—about 3–4 minutes on each side. Remove pan from heat, lightly salt and pepper breasts, and put a slice of cheese over each. Set skillet under broiler until cheese melts.

Serve chicken with rice and stewed tomatoes, peas, succotash, or baby carrots.

Serves 4.

CUCUMBER DELIGHT

2 cucumbers, peeled and sliced
½ cup yogurt
3 tablespoons mayonnaise
1 teaspoon lemon juice
½ teaspoon dried dill
Salt and pepper to taste

Toss all ingredients together lightly.

Serves 4.

HEAVENLY HASH

    2 tablespoons vegetable oil
    1 lb ground round
    1 small onion, finely chopped
    6 large mushrooms, sliced
    1 cup sour cream
       Salt and pepper to taste

Heat oil in a heavy skillet. Crumble meat into pan and sauté rapidly. When meat has lost pink color, add onion and cook until soft.

Stir in mushrooms and cook 1–2 minutes more. Mix in sour cream, salt, and pepper, and heat through.

Serve this rich treat over rice, noodles, or toasted English muffins. The salad below and some iced tea go well with this meal.

Serves 4.

CRASH CASSOULET

    3 tablespoons butter
    1 bunch scallions, chopped
    2 garlic cloves, finely chopped (optional)
    4 knockwurst or frankfurters, or ½ kielbasa, sliced into rings
    2 cans (20-oz size) cannellini (white beans)

Put a large heavy skillet on top of stove and heat butter. Add scallions, garlic, and knockwurst, and cook about 7 minutes, stirring occasionally. Add cannellini. Cover skillet and allow to simmer for 5 minutes more or until beans are hot.

Round out meal with some pumpernickel bread, pickles, and lemonade or beer.

Serves 4.

MOCK REUBEN SANDWICHES

    1 lb sauerkraut
    6 frankfurters or knockwurst
    ¼ teaspoon caraway seeds (optional)
    4 slices family-sized rye bread
       Butter
    8 slices Swiss or Muenster cheese

Preheat broiler. Drain sauerkraut and put in a saucepan with frankfurters. Add caraway seeds, cover, and simmer for 5–7 minutes, or until meat is heated through.

Toast and butter rye bread. Lay a piece of aluminum foil in a baking pan or on a cookie sheet and arrange toast on foil.

Remove sauerkraut and meat to a colander, and while sauerkraut drains again, slice sausages lengthwise into 2 or 3 pieces. Arrange meat on pieces of toast and divide sauerkraut over them. Top with cheese. Put open-face sandwiches under broiler until cheese is melted and browned, about 2–3 minutes.

To round out meal, add mustard or Russian dressing, kosher dill pickles, cold beer or cider, and chilled applesauce for dessert.

Serves 3–4.

BEST RECIPES FOR FRANKS AND BURGERS

Plump hamburgers dripping juice onto a sizzling fire. Hot dogs grilled to perfection and served on toasty buns. Memories of this royal feast linger with anyone who has enjoyed an all-American cookout. But you don't need a bonfire to create a savory meal with hot dogs and hamburgers—only a stovetop burner and, of course, a hungry family and a willing mom or dad. For a delicious change of pace, we offer recipes for international dishes based on these two favorites.

First, some basic cooking tips. There seem to be as many methods of making hamburgers as there are people who like to fix them. Most would agree, however, on this rule of thumb: Handle the meat as little as possible before cooking; too much handling makes the hamburgers tough. Some chefs recommend gently mixing a lightly beaten raw egg into the meat to bind it together before cooking. Then they sear the patties quickly on both sides in a little butter or oil and cook over moderate heat until the meat is done. If the beef isn't lean, don't cook it in butter or oil; just sprinkle a little salt into the frying pan before you put the hamburger patties in.

There's no trick to fixing hot dogs—either you boil, broil, or fry them. (To get more of the lovely, crispy outside part when broiling or frying the hot dogs, slash them lengthwise.)

While you cook the meat, let the kids help prepare the salad or side dishes. Then, when dinner is served, listen to the whole family speak this universal language: Mmmmmm!

GYPSY-STYLE HOT DOGS
SPINACH SALAD
BLUEBERRIES WITH YOGURT

Cooked in one pot—gypsy style—this flavorful dish is just the thing for an easy, no-fuss meal.

GYPSY-STYLE HOT DOGS

        1 medium onion, sliced
        1 green pepper, chopped
        ¾ lb mushrooms, sliced
        2 teaspoons olive oil
        1 lb hot dogs, cut into bite-size chunks
        1 can (12-oz size) tomatoes, chopped
        1 cup dry white wine
    1½ cups water
        1 cup uncooked rice
        1 teaspoon oregano
           Salt and pepper to taste

In a large frying pan, sauté onion, pepper, and mushrooms in olive oil for about 5 minutes.

Add hot dogs, tomatoes, wine, water, rice, and seasonings, and stir. Bring mixture to a boil.

Reduce heat and cover. Simmer for about 25 minutes, or until rice is done.

Serves 4.

SPINACH SALAD

        1 lb fresh spinach, washed
        2 hard-boiled eggs, coarsely chopped
        1 large tomato, cut into 8 wedges
        ¼ cup chopped scallions
        6 strips bacon, cooked and crumbled

Dressing:
        ¼ cup olive oil
        3 tablespoons lemon juice
        ½ teaspoon salt
           Pepper to taste

Combine spinach, eggs, tomato, scallions, and bacon in a large bowl.

Combine dressing ingredients in a jar with a lid. Cover and shake well. Pour dressing over salad and toss.

Serves 4.

STEAKBURGERS WITH MUSHROOM SAUCE
FRENCH BREAD
SLICED TOMATOES
LEMON SHERBET

These lean, garlicky burgers covered with an aromatic sauce are extra juicy.

STEAKBURGERS WITH MUSHROOM SAUCE

    1 lb chopped round or sirloin beef
    1 clove garlic, minced
    ¾ teaspoon dry mustard
    1 tablespoon oil
      Salt and pepper to taste
    3 tablespoons butter
    1 tablespoon lemon juice
    2 tablespoons chopped scallions
    3 tablespoons dry white wine
    ¾ teaspoon Worcestershire sauce
    ½ lb mushrooms, sliced

Form the chopped meat into 4 burgers. Sprinkle on each side with garlic and mustard.

Put oil in a large skillet. When very hot, add burgers. Fry over high heat for about 5 minutes, or until browned on each side. Transfer burgers to a plate, and salt and pepper lightly.

Add butter, lemon juice, and scallions to skillet and bring to a boil, stirring. Add wine and Worcestershire sauce, and stir. Add mushrooms. Simmer several minutes, stirring constantly, until sauce has reduced slightly. Spoon sauce over burgers and serve with bread. Or for gourmet steak sandwiches, serve burgers between two pieces of buttered French bread.

Serves 4.

HOT DOGS WITH THE ULTIMATE BARBECUE SAUCE
NEW-POTATO SALAD
CARROT STICKS
WATERMELON

Sweet and zesty barbecue sauce from scratch is a snap to make. Cooking the hot dogs in the sauce makes them extra flavorful and your preparation extra easy. If the potato salad seems like too much trouble, substitute corn on the cob.

HOT DOGS WITH THE ULTIMATE BARBECUE SAUCE

       1 medium onion, finely chopped
       1 can (16-oz size) tomato puree
       2 cloves garlic, crushed
     ¼ cup sherry
       1 tablespoon honey
         Dash of Tabasco
     ½ teaspoon dry mustard
       1 teaspoon dried basil
       2 teaspoons chili powder
       1 teaspoon salt
         Pepper to taste
       1 lb hot dogs
         Hard rolls or hot-dog buns

Put all ingredients except hot dogs and rolls in a large saucepan and bring to a boil.

Reduce heat and cover. Simmer for 30 minutes, stirring occasionally, until thickened. Add hot dogs and simmer for 10–15 minutes more. Remove hot dogs from sauce. Serve immediately on rolls. Pass sauce.

Serves 4.

NEW-POTATO SALAD

       1 lb new potatoes, washed
     ¼ cup chopped scallions
       3 tablespoons chopped fresh dill
     ¼ cup mayonnaise
       1 tablespoon spicy mustard
       1 teaspoon salt

Boil potatoes (do not peel) in 4 cups of water for about 25 minutes, or until a fork slides easily into potatoes. Drain and cool. Leave on skins and cut into bite-size chunks.

Combine scallions, dill, mayonnaise, mustard, and salt.

Toss potato chunks with mayonnaise mixture. Serve salad warm or chilled.

Serves 4–6.

PERSIAN BURGERS IN PITAS
EGGPLANT SALAD
HONEYDEW MELON

Herbs and spices make an ordinary burger exotic. From the many splendors of Middle Eastern cooking comes this aromatic burger, scented with delicate summer mint—and the magic of Arabian Nights! (For a change, try ground lamb instead of beef.)

PERSIAN BURGERS IN PITAS

- 2 medium sprigs fresh mint
- 1 lb ground beef
- ½ medium onion, finely chopped
- ½ teaspoon allspice
- 1 teaspoon salt
- 1 egg
- ¼ cup pine nuts (optional)
- 1 tablespoon oil
- 4 pitas
  Shredded lettuce

Strip mint leaves from stalks and chop coarsely.

In a bowl, combine beef, onion, allspice, salt, egg, mint leaves, and pine nuts. Mold mixture into 4 patties.

Heat oil in a medium skillet. Fry burgers over medium heat for 10–15 minutes, turning once or twice. Serve immediately in pitas with shredded lettuce.

Serves 4.

EGGPLANT SALAD

> 1 medium eggplant
> ¼ cup olive oil
> 1 cup chopped tomatoes
> 1 cup chopped scallions
> ¼ cup lemon juice
> 1 teaspoon salt
> ¼ teaspoon cayenne pepper

Peel eggplant and cut into small cubes.

Heat oil in a frying pan. When hot, add eggplant, tomatoes, and scallions, and sauté over low heat for 10 minutes, stirring often.

When eggplant is tender, turn eggplant, tomatoes, and scallions into a large bowl. Add lemon juice, salt, and cayenne pepper. Mix well. Serve warm or chilled.

Serves 4–6.

HOT DOGS CHOUCROUTE ON TOASTED BUNS
GREEN SALAD VINAIGRETTE
POUND CAKE WITH CHOCOLATE ICE CREAM

This tasty takeoff on the famous Alsatian sausage dish is sure to satisfy every sauerkraut lover!

HOT DOGS CHOUCROUTE

> 1 package (16-oz size) sauerkraut
> 2 cloves garlic, crushed
> 1 medium onion, sliced
> 1 cup dry white wine
> ½ teaspoon ground cloves
>   Salt and pepper to taste
> 1 lb hot dogs
>   Hot dog buns

Put sauerkraut, garlic, onion, wine, cloves, salt, and pepper in a Dutch oven on top of stove. Stir, then add hot dogs. Bring to a boil and reduce heat. Cover and simmer for 30 minutes.

Toast buns. Arrange a hot dog and some sauerkraut on each bun. Serves 4.

GUACAMOLE HAMBURGERS
CUCUMBER STICKS AND MUSHROOMS
YOGURT DIP
FRESH PINEAPPLE CHUNKS

Kids will love this "hands-on" supper. To jazz up dessert for the grownups, pour some crème de menthe or Grand Marnier liqueur over the pineapple.

GUACAMOLE HAMBURGERS

    1 lb ground beef
    1 tablespoon butter
    1 large ripe avocado, peeled, pitted, and halved
    1 large tomato, chopped
    ½ small onion, chopped
    3 tablespoons lime juice
    ¼ teaspoon salt
       Pepper to taste
    1 package (7-oz size) taco shells

Mold beef into 12 small patties.

Melt butter in a large frying pan and sauté burgers over low heat for about 10 minutes, turning often so they cook evenly.

While burgers are cooking, make guacamole: Puree avocado, tomato, onion, lime juice, salt, and pepper in a blender or food processor.

Serve burgers in taco shells with large dollops of guacamole.

Serves 4.

YOGURT DIP

    1 cup plain yogurt
    ½ small onion, finely chopped
    2 cloves garlic, crushed
    ½ teaspoon salt
    2 tablespoons chopped fresh dill
    1 tablespoon lemon juice

Combine all ingredients. Stir to mix thoroughly.

Cover and chill until serving time.

Serves 4.

CHAPTER FIVE
BREAKFASTS
OVER EASY

Heaven knows it's hard enough to get yourself out the door in the morning without trying to produce a big breakfast. But if you would like a change from your usual fare—and have a bit of extra time— try one of these suggestions.

Carrots and Nuts: Split and toast a bagel. Spread with chunky peanut butter. Slice a carrot into rounds and press into peanut butter. Serves 1.

Tomato-Egg Wake-up: In a blender, combine 2 eggs, 2 cups of tomato juice, ¼ teaspoon of Worcestershire sauce, and a dash of Tabasco. Blend until frothy. Pour into glasses. Serves 2.

Bananas on a Raft: Toast 2 slices of whole wheat bread. While toast is still hot, spread with honey. Slice a banana and press into honey. Spoon some vanilla yogurt onto each slice and eat with knife and fork. Serves 2.

Fruit Smoothy: In a blender, combine 1 small can of undrained fruit cocktail, 1 cup of milk, ½ cup of plain yogurt, a dash of nutmeg, and 4 ice cubes. Process until smooth and pour into glasses. Serves 2.

A Nutty Sandwich: Split and toast an English muffin. Spread one half with cream cheese and press some peanuts into cheese. Spread other half with apple butter; press halves together to form a sandwich. Serves 1.

Hot and Creamy Cereal: Prepare 3 servings of hot rice cereal according to package directions. When cereal is almost done, add 3 tablespoons of raisins. Spoon cereal into bowls and pour on some maple syrup. For a super-rich treat, top with heavy cream. Serves 3.

Glazed Ham on Toast: Toast 3 slices of whole wheat bread and spread with orange marmalade. Top each slice with 1 or 2 slices of ham. Serves 3.

Fiery Eggs: Scramble 6 eggs with a handful of bean sprouts and a dash of Tabasco. Serve with hot corn muffins. Serves 3.

Hot Fruit-and-Nut Yogurt: In a saucepan over medium heat, cook 2 cups of dried fruit (apricots, prunes, raisins, and apples are nice) with ¾ cup of apple or orange juice until liquid is slightly absorbed by fruit —about 3–4 minutes. Turn into 3 bowls and top each with several big spoonfuls of vanilla or plain yogurt and a handful of chopped nuts. Stir. Serves 3.

Butterscotch Muffins: Cream 3 tablespoons of butter with 1½ tablespoons of brown sugar. Split 3 bran muffins; spread each half with butter mixture. Sprinkle with cinnamon and put under broiler for 2–3 minutes. Place a slice of farmer cheese on each bottom half and cover with top half. Serves 3.

Melon Smoothies: In a blender, combine 1 cup of cantaloupe cubes, 1 cup of sliced strawberries, 1 cup of plain or vanilla yogurt, and 1 cup of milk. Process until smooth. Pour into glasses. Serves 2–3.

Cold Cereal with Extra Zip: For variety, combine 2 or 3 kinds of dry cereal in each person's bowl, sprinkle on a little wheat germ and brown sugar, and pour milk over all.

Cheesy Eggs: Soft-boil 6 eggs. Crack open into cups and dot yolks with a little butter. Sprinkle with paprika and grated Parmesan cheese. Pass a plate of buttered rye toast. Serves 3–6.

Crunchy Muffins: In a bowl, combine 1 cup of crunchy peanut butter with 2 tablespoons of granola, 1 tablespoon of wheat germ, and ¼ cup of shredded coconut. Serve on buttered English muffins. Serves 5.

Walnut-Raisin Toast: Spread cream cheese on 5 slices of toasted raisin bread. Press several walnut halves into cream cheese on each slice. Serve with quartered oranges. Serves 5.

Tropical Shake: In a blender, combine 1 egg, ½ cup of milk, and 1 cup of pineapple-orange yogurt. Blend until frothy. Pour into a tall glass. Serves 1.

Grits with Soul: Empty a packet of instant grits into a bowl and stir in ½ cup of boiling water. Add 1 teaspoon of grated Parmesan or Romano cheese and 1 teaspoon of butter. Stir in a little milk or cream if desired. Some fruit on the side—say, a bunch of green grapes—would complete this quick meal. Serves 1.

Appealing Bananas: Slice 4 peeled bananas on diagonal. Heat 2 tablespoons of butter or margarine in a skillet and sauté bananas, turning once. Sprinkle on some cinnamon-sugar and divide into 4 bowls. Add a dollop of yogurt or sour cream to each helping. Serves 4.

Cheery Cereal: Half-fill 4 bowls with your family's favorite cereal. Core and thinly slice (but do not peel) 2 rosy-red apples and divide slices over cereal. Sprinkle some peanuts over each helping and add a little granulated brown sugar and milk or half-and-half. Serves 4.

Hotshot Eggs: Break 4 or 5 eggs into a bowl and beat well. Heat 2 tablespoons of butter, margarine, or vegetable oil in a skillet over medium heat and add eggs. Stir in ½ cup of seasoned croutons and scramble eggs. Divide eggs onto 3 or 4 plates and add 1–2 dashes of Tabasco to each helping. Pass buttered rye toast. Serves 3–4.

Hawaiian Toast: Butter several pieces of whole wheat bread. Put them on a foil-covered cookie sheet or baking pan. Stack a slice each of ham and mild cheese (such as Muenster) on bread and top with a ring of canned pineapple. Put under broiler until cheese melts. Serve with a combination of orange and pineapple juice.

Swiss Toast: Lightly toast and butter some rye bread, and cover each piece with a slice of Swiss cheese. Top cheese with a few slivers of apple and sprinkle with cinnamon and sugar. Place toast on a foil-covered cookie sheet or baking pan and put under broiler until cheese melts. Serve with hot apple cider or apple juice.

Sweet Cereal: To your family's favorite bran cereal, add a mixture of chopped dried apricots, walnuts, prunes, and brown sugar. Serve cereal as usual with milk. For a beverage, try your favorite tea sweetened with a teaspoon of blackberry or currant jelly instead of sugar.

Fruity Creamy Treat: Prepare Cream of Wheat or farina according to directions on package. In another saucepan, melt ½ teaspoon butter, 1 tablespoon of apricot preserves, and 1 squeeze of lemon per person. Pour apricot sauce over each serving of cereal and pass around some cream or half-and-half. Herbal tea goes nicely with this rich breakfast.

Breakfast Kabobs: Prepare these the night before and pop them in broiler the next morning. Place brown-and-serve sausages alternating with canned pineapple chunks on skewers. Cover and refrigerate. Next morning, uncover and place under broiler. Turn once and broil until sausages are nicely browned. Breakfast kabobs are delicious served with toasted English muffins.

Saucy Poached Eggs: Combine 1 can of condensed cream soup (mushroom, celery, and chicken are good) and ½ cup of milk in a medium skillet. Add a dash of prepared mustard or a tablespoon of Parmesan cheese, if desired. Bring to boiling; reduce heat to simmer. Poach in soup 1 or 2 eggs for each member of your family: Crack eggs 1 at a time onto saucer and gently slide into soup. Cover pan and let simmer until eggs are the way you like them—2–4 minutes. Lift each egg onto a piece of toast and spoon some sauce over top.

Pita Plus: Slice leftover meat, such as chicken, ham, or pot roast, into juilienne strips. Sauté in butter until warmed through. Add a beaten egg and a little salt and pepper. Cook as you would scrambled eggs. Spoon mixture into a warm pita. For more than 1 serving, add more eggs and cook all at once. This makes a great eat-on-the-way breakfast for those mornings when the whole family is running late.

Hot Apple Cereal: Put ¾ cup of thinly sliced apple into a medium saucepan. Add amount of water specified on package for 3 servings of your favorite instant hot cereal. Bring to boiling, then simmer for 3 minutes. Stir in cereal and follow package directions on waiting time. Divide into 4 serving dishes. Top with brown sugar and warm milk.

Pancakes You Don't Have to Flip Over: Preheat oven to 350° F. Using your favorite pancake mix, make enough batter for 4 servings. Pour into a greased 9-by-13-inch baking pan and place in oven. Finish dressing, pack lunches, or listen to your children's spelling words one more time. You have 10–12 minutes—pancake is done when top feels firm. Cut into squares and serve, bottom-side up, with butter and syrup or an assortment of preserves.

Mock Tropical Treat: Combine a container of orange-pineapple or banana yogurt with ½ cup of spoon-size shredded wheat. (Crush shredded wheat, if you like.) Sprinkle mixture liberally with flaked coconut.

Breakfast Frittata: Beat 3 eggs with 6 tablespoons of milk until well blended. Fold in ¼ cup of cubed ham or luncheon meat, 1 cup of cubed fresh bread, and 2 tablespoons of grated Parmesan cheese. In a 9-inch skillet, melt 1 tablespoon of butter, making sure entire bottom of skillet is coated. Pour in egg mixture and cook, covered, over low heat until top feels firm—10–12 minutes. Invert onto serving plate and cut into wedges. Serves 2–3.

Strawberry Sandwich Surprise: Toast 8 frozen waffles. Spread 4 with honey and then spoon on some sour cream or plain or vanilla yogurt. Top with sliced strawberries and cover with another waffle. Serves 4.

Hawaiian Scrambled Eggs: Break 5 eggs into a mixing bowl and beat with 2 tablespoons of pineapple juice and a dash of nutmeg. Mix in ½ of a small can of drained, crushed pineapple. Cook eggs as usual. Sprinkle with flaked coconut, if desired. Pass around a plate of buttered toast. Serves 3.

Protein Shake: In a blender, combine 2½ cups of milk, 2 small sliced bananas, 2 heaping teaspoons of smooth peanut butter, 2 teaspoons of honey, and a dash of cinnamon. Blend on high speed. Serves 2.

Cold Cereal with a Special Touch: Instead of using sugar, spoon a big dollop of applesauce into a bowl of your favorite cold cereal with milk or cream.

Muffin Treat: Split and toast 4 cinnamon-raisin English muffins and spread with cream cheese. Pass around an assortment of preserves and some chopped walnuts. Serves 4.

Jammy Flakes: Pour your favorite corn or oat flakes into a bowl. Melt 2 generous spoonfuls of jam in a small saucepan over low heat. Drizzle warm jam over cereal. Pour on some milk or half-and-half.

Orange Eggnog: In a blender container, combine ½ can (6-oz size) of frozen orange juice concentrate, 2 cups of milk, 2 eggs, and 1 teaspoon of vanilla. Blend until frothy. Pour into glasses. Serves 2.

Eggs with Sprouts: Heat a dab of butter or margarine in a skillet. In a small bowl, whisk 2 eggs with 2 tablespoons of water and 1 tablespoon of grated Parmesan cheese; pour into skillet. Sprinkle with a handful of alfalfa sprouts and cover pan. Cook over low heat until eggs are set. Roll up and slide from pan into a warmed hot-dog bun. Serves 1.

Pineapple and Cheese: Split and toast an English muffin. Spread both halves with cream cheese. Spoon crushed pineapple on each half and sprinkle with cinnamon. Slide under broiler and cook for 3–4 minutes, until cheese is bubbly. Serves 1–2.

Ricotta Cone: You overslept? Put a scoop of ricotta or cottage cheese in an ice-cream cone and stud with raisins and peanuts. Hand your child his breakfast on his way out the door!

Apricot Antics: Split and toast a bagel. Meanwhile, combine 2 tablespoons of cream cheese, 1 tablespoon of honey, and a pinch of nutmeg. Spread bagel with cheese mixture and press a few dried apricots into cheese. Serves 1.

Special Fried Egg: Use a drinking glass to cut a hole in the center of a slice of bread. Heat a tablespoon of butter in a skillet, add bread, and crack an egg into hole. Cook over medium heat until egg is set. Slide egg and bread onto a plate. Top with a tomato slice. Serves 1.

Nuts and Dates: In a small bowl, combine 2 tablespoons of peanut butter with 1 tablespoon of honey and a dash of cinnamon. Spread on toasted whole wheat bread. Chop 1 or 2 dates and press into peanut butter. Serves 1.

Yogurt Parfait: Spoon vanilla yogurt into a tall glass or sundae dish. Sprinkle on some bran cereal or wheat germ. Add a layer of sliced apples or orange wedges. Repeat with another layer of everything.

Banana Toast: Toast 2 slices of raisin bread. Meanwhile, mash a small banana with 2 tablespoons of peanut butter and spread mixture on toast. Sprinkle with chopped nuts. Serves 1–2.

Iced Chocolate: Put 1 cup of milk, 1 egg, 1 teaspoon of unsweetened cocoa, 1 teaspoon of honey, 1 sliced banana, and 2 ice cubes into a blender container. Whirl until frothy. Serves 1.

Crunchy Lemon Pancakes: To a thawed container (16-oz size) of frozen pancake batter, add grated rind of 1 lemon and 2 tablespoons of wheat germ. Cook as usual. Serve with butter and honey or syrup. Serves 4–5.

Sunny Cereal: To a bowl of your favorite dry cereal, add some orange sections and a handful of raisins. Pour on cold milk.

Veggie Cocktail: Put 1 cup of tomato juice, ¼ cup of plain yogurt, 1 stalk of celery, chopped, 2 ice cubes, and a dash of Worcestershire sauce into a blender container. Whirl until frothy. Serves 1.

Spanish Eggs: In a skillet, sauté about ⅓ cup of chopped green pepper in a little butter. Add 1 small can of stewed tomatoes and cook for 2 minutes more. Beat 6 eggs and pour into skillet (do not mix). Cook over medium heat until set. Serves 3.

Fruit Mélange: Slice a cantaloupe in half and scoop out seeds. Fill each hollow with plain or vanilla yogurt and some raisins or chopped nuts. Serves 2.

Pita Pockets: Scramble 2 eggs with a little chopped parsley or chives. Toast a pita, slice it open, and stuff with eggs.

Breakfast Melt: Split and toast 2 English muffins. Top each muffin half with 1 slice of ham, 1 slice of tomato, and 1 slice of mozzarella cheese. Run under broiler to melt cheese. Serves 2–4.

Corn Pancakes: Blend 1 cup of flour, 1½ teaspoons of baking powder, 1 egg, ¾ cup of milk, and a 7-ounce can of whole-kernel corn, drained. Ladle batter onto a hot, greased griddle. When pancakes are lightly browned, flip them over. Serve with maple syrup. Serves 2–3.

Bacon 'n' Cheese: Split and toast 2 pumpernickel bagels. Top with cheddar-cheese spread. Sprinkle each half with chopped scallions and crumbled crisp bacon. Serves 2.

Mexican Eggs: Beat 6 eggs with 3 tablespoons of chili sauce. Scramble as usual. Garnish each serving with a dollop of sour cream. Pass some buttered rye toast. Serves 3.

Super Cider: Heat 1 cup of cider, 1 cup of orange juice, and ¼ teaspoon of cinnamon in a small saucepan. Pour into 2 mugs. Serve with whole wheat toast spread with peanut butter. Serves 2.

Waffles Supreme: Toast a batch of frozen waffles and smother each one with butter or margarine. Spoon on some honey and sliced fresh peaches.

Fruity Rice Pudding: Dish out some canned rice pudding for everyone and pass around bowls of sliced fresh plums and bananas. Each person can stir either or both fruits into the pudding and then drench mixture with heavy cream. A dash of nutmeg completes the treat.

Variations on Toast, à la Pennsylvania Dutch: Lightly butter thick slices of whole wheat toast and spread each slice with a generous dollop of apple butter. Top each piece with slivers of cheddar cheese. Slip bread under broiler to melt cheese. A simpler version: Spread each slice of toast with cream cheese and spoon apple butter on top.

Egg on Toast: Arrange slices of hard-boiled egg on buttered toast and top with crumbled bacon.

Sautéed Apples: Core and slice an apple. Melt some butter or margarine in a frying pan over medium heat and lightly sauté apple slices until golden brown. While fruit is cooking, split leftover dinner biscuits and warm them in oven. Remove biscuits to a plate, slide apple slices onto biscuits, and drizzle with maple syrup.

CEREAL BARS

  1 cup sugar
  ½ cup soft butter or margarine
  1 cup applesauce
1¾ cups flour
  1 teaspoon baking soda
  1 teaspoon cinnamon
  ¼ teaspoon salt
  1 cup raisins
  ¼ cup chopped walnuts
  ¼ cup wheat germ

Topping:
  1 cup dry cereal flakes
  ¼ cup sugar
  ¼ cup chopped walnuts
  2 tablespoons butter

Preheat oven to 350° F. Grease a 9-by-13-inch baking pan. Cream sugar and butter, and stir in applesauce. Mix remaining ingredients and stir into batter. Pour into pan. Combine topping ingredients and sprinkle over batter. Bake for 20–25 minutes. Cool and cut into bars.

TUTTI-FRUTTI SHAKE

A fruit milk shake is perfect with toast or peanut butter sandwiches that the kids can make themselves.

1 cup milk
1 egg
½ cup sliced fruit, such as peaches
1 teaspoon honey
  Dash of vanilla

Combine ingredients in a blender and mix very well. Serves 1.

When you have a few nearly-empty boxes of different breakfast cereals, pour contents of all into one big bowl, mix with yogurt and raisins, and serve.

Don't throw out those very ripe bananas, no matter how soft or bruised. Make banana milk shakes: In a blender, combine bananas, honey, a raw egg for each family member, milk, and a dash of vanilla. Serve with toasted English muffins topped with peanut butter and jelly.

If you're all in a hurry, spoon some honey and cereal onto plain yogurt. Serve with steaming mugs of hot chocolate, and everybody will be set to go.

Health fans will love melted Muenster cheese topped with alfalfa sprouts on toasted English muffins.

Bowls of cereal with sliced bananas, sliced apples, and milk make a great first meal of the day. Serve with peach nectar; it's so rich it seems like a breakfast in itself.

Tempt your family with French toast: For eight pieces, beat two eggs, one cup of milk, a dash of vanilla, and some cinnamon. Dip slices of wheat bread in this liquid and fry in a combination of hot butter and vegetable oil. If any pieces are left over after breakfast, wrap individually in foil and freeze. In the morning, pop in the toaster.

Youngsters love graham crackers spread with peanut butter and topped with raisins or coconut. You and your husband might prefer a sprinkling of crumbled bacon or shredded carrots.

Scramble some eggs with diced leftover chicken, ham, or whatever. They're delicious with buttered toast and chilled grapefruit juice.

Toast and butter English muffins and spread with applesauce topped with yogurt, wheat germ, and cinnamon.

Liven up hard-boiled eggs and carrot strips with a dab of mayonnaise; butter some toasted rye bread; and pour everyone a glass of vegetable juice.

Canned peaches, pears, or plums served with a dollop of sour cream and a liberal sprinkling of bran cereal make a tasty, light breakfast.

Pour half-and-half over mashed bananas and sprinkle with wheat flakes and brown sugar. This rich dish is delicious with cups of hot herb tea.

Instant hot cereal is instant goodness on a cold morning. Because it comes in individual packets, each person can fix it just the way he or she wants—with fruit, milk, honey, brown sugar, or even molasses.

Spread toasted rye or whole wheat bread with cottage cheese and top with fresh orange or apple slices, or some strawberry or apricot jam.

Half grapefruits and buttered corn muffins make a quick, delicious breakfast when everyone has to dash out early.

CHAPTER SIX

WHAT'S FOR LUNCH?

Maybe the kids are happy eating a peanut butter and jelly sandwich every day for lunch, but most adults prefer a little variety. Here are some simple suggestions for making your midday meal a delicious treat.

Spicy tacos (sliced chicken, shredded iceberg lettuce, and a dollop of barbecue sauce in a taco shell)
Potato chips
Shortbread cookie

Sandwich of Muenster cheese, sunflower seeds, and mustard on an onion bagel
Black olives
Container of canned peaches

Container of exotic tuna salad (crumbled tuna, chopped scallions, and marinated artichoke hearts tossed with red wine vinegar and oil dressing)
Buttered hard roll
Dates

Container of colorful carrot salad (shredded carrots mixed with avocado and tomato slices and French dressing)
Whole wheat crackers
Banana

Sandwich of sliced ham, chopped fresh spinach, and Russian dressing in a pita
Broccoli florets
Tangerine

Container of salmon salad (canned salmon mixed with chopped celery and hard-boiled egg, sweet pickle relish, and mayonnaise)
Soda crackers
Apple

Sandwich of peanut butter and pear slices on oatmeal bread
Termos of vegetable soup
Chocolate chip cookie

Container of deli salad (pepperoni strips, garbanzo beans, grated Parmesan cheese, and Boston lettuce tossed with Italian dressing)
Orange

Container of Oriental salad (cooked brown rice mixed with pineapple chunks, green peas, and teriyaki sauce)
Grapefruit sections

Container of coffee yogurt mixed with chopped pecans and dried apricots
Raw string beans
Bran muffin

Thermos of lentil soup
Sandwich of sliced Lebanon bologna, horseradish, and catsup on a hamburger bun
Sweet midget gherkins
Shortbread cookie

Sandwich of sliced brick cheese, Bermuda onion, and brown mustard on pumpernickel bread
Raw string beans
Chocolate chip cookie

Thermos of vegetable soup
Wedge of Gouda cheese
Sesame crackers
Pear

Container of crunchy salad (cherry tomatoes, chopped green pepper, and drained canned corn mixed with Italian dressing)
Buttered hard roll
Carrot cake
Apple juice

Sandwich of egg salad, bacon bits, and bean sprouts in a pita pocket
Cauliflorets
Canned fruit cocktail

Container of pasta salad (broccoli florets, cherry tomatoes, chopped scallions, and cooked macaroni mixed with blue cheese dressing)
Apple

Sandwich of peanut butter, raisins, and sliced bananas on a bagel
Carrot sticks
Oatmeal cookie

Thermos of tomato soup
Container of cottage cheese with garden vegetables
Blueberry muffin
Pistacho nuts

Sandwich of Mexican tuna fish salad (tuna fish mixed with chopped green chili peppers, diced onions, tomato, and a little mayonnaise) in a taco shell or pita
Grapes
Orange juice

Container of carrot-raisin salad (shredded carrots mixed with raisins and chopped walnuts) topped with a slice of farmer cheese
Bran muffin
Apple juice

Sandwich of salmon (canned) mixed with vinaigrette dressing and alfalfa sprouts on a bagel
Raw string beans
Banana
Hot herb tea

Container of cottage cheese mixed with chopped marinated artichoke hearts
Cheese-flavored bread sticks
Apple
Tomato juice with a squeeze of lemon

Sandwich of herbed cream cheese (cream cheese mashed with chopped parsley and a dash of dried dill) with tomato slices and spinach leaves on French bread
Wedge of melon
Grapefruit juice

Large container filled with cantaloupe pieces, cashew nuts, and grapes mixed with lemon yogurt
Carrot sticks
Melba toast
Club soda

Container of strawberries topped with a piece of farmer cheese and a dash of nutmeg
Bran muffin
Cauliflorets
Vegetable juice

Sandwich of sliced avocado and Muenster cheese with Russian dressing on whole wheat bread
Cherries
Iced tea

Fresh broccoli spears with a squeeze of lemon
Brie or other soft cheese on a sliced bagel
Grapefruit juice

Sandwich of garbanzos (¾ cup of canned garbanzo beans, mashed
   with a dash of lemon juice) with ½ cup of applesauce and a dash of
   cinnamon in a pita
Peach
Tomato juice

Sandwich of Chinese chicken salad (1 small can of chunk-style chicken,
   drained, mashed with 1 tablespoon of mayonnaise and 1 teaspoon of
   soy sauce) with lettuce on a hard roll
Cherry tomatoes
Lemonade

Container of raw zucchini slices, mushrooms, and string beans
Container of dip (¼ cup of sour cream combined with ¼ cup of yogurt;
   seasoned to taste with pepper and onion salt)
Plum
Cranberry juice

Zucchini dog (zucchini, split lengthwise, hollowed out and stuffed with
   a mixture of tuna salad and diced red pepper)
Whole wheat pretzels
Apple juice

Sandwich of thinly sliced apple and Cheddar cheese on lightly buttered
   raisin bread
Cranberry juice

Sardines and cream cheese on whole wheat bread (one slice spread with
   cream cheese, with sardines mashed with a little lemon juice on top;
   can be eaten as an open sandwich or topped with another slice of
   bread)
Raisins
Iced tea

Container of melon balls, mandarin orange sections, and almond slivers
   with a scoop of lemon yogurt and a sprinkle of cinnamon
Bran muffin
Iced coffee

Shish kabobs (wooden skewers or toothpicks with cheese cubes, chunks
   of cooked beef or chicken, pineapple chunks, cherry tomatoes, and
   green pepper pieces)
Vegetable cocktail juice

Sandwich of peanut butter and bacon bits on a bagel
Grapes
Apricot nectar

Thinly sliced French bread
Slices of salami and Swiss cheese
Small sweet pickles
Nectarine
Bottled sparkling water

Avocado half stuffed with tuna salad (a bit of lemon juice squeezed on
   avocado prevents discoloration and tastes delicious)
Celery sticks
Pineapple juice

Pita bread stuffed with Muenster cheese, green pepper, bean sprouts, and
   creamy garlic dressing
Thermos of hot tomato soup or carton of orange juice

Sandwich of chopped liver with tomato and Swiss cheese on a bagel
Grapes
Bottled sparkling water

Container of cold asparagus spears with a little oil and vinegar and a
   scoop of spring-garden cottage cheese
Melba toast
Cantaloupe section
Herb tea

Hero sandwich of provolone cheese, salami, pimiento, and black olive
   slices on whole wheat Italian bread
Tangerine
Iced tea

Sandwich of walnuts and cream cheese on raisin bread
Banana
Thermos of hot alphabet vegetable soup

Sandwich of peanut butter, sliced bananas, and honey on whole wheat
   bread
Dried pineapple slices
Carton of milk

Container of cold cooked broccoli spears topped with hard-boiled egg
   slices and a little vinaigrette dressing
Sesame bread sticks
Thermos of hot or chilled cream of celery soup

Pita bread stuffed with shredded red cabbage, carrot, Jarlsberg cheese, chickpeas, and black olives
Dried coconut pieces
Orange juice

Sandwich of liverwurst with tomato on Italian bread
Container of fruit salad
Hot or iced coffee

Container of spinach salad with tomato and mushroom slices, shredded Swiss cheese, and bean sprouts, dressed with oil and vinegar
Dried pear slices
Iced tea

Avocado and Muenster cheese on cracked wheat bread (one slice spread with mashed avocado, put shredded cheese on top; can be eaten as an open sandwich or topped with another slice of lightly buttered bread)
Thermos of hot chicken broth
Orange

Sandwich of Jarlsberg cheese and green pepper pieces with mayonnaise on onion herb bread
Nut and raisin mixture
Orange juice

Sandwich of cream cheese and pitted olives (green or black) on pumpernickel bread
Orange or grapes
Cranapple juice

Container of sliced fresh mushrooms and diced Gruyère cheese, with oil and vinegar dressing
Thermos of hot chicken broth
Cantaloupe slices
Mint tea

Thermos of hot vegetable soup
Hard roll and butter
Apple wedges with slices of cheddar cheese
Hot coffee

Stuffed tomato (hollowed-out tomato filled with cottage cheese mixed with chives, raisins, and grated carrots)
Banana bread
Slice of honeydew melon
Tomato juice

Fruit salad of apples, oranges, bananas, grapes, and berries laced with orange juice
Buttered corn muffin
Hard-boiled egg
Mineral water

Pita bread stuffed with Greek salad of shredded lettuce, diced cucumber and tomato, pitted black olives, and crumbled feta cheese
Container of oil and vinegar dressing
Orange
Hot chocolate

Apple and small box of raisins
Container of peanut butter (at lunchtime: Slice up apple, spread peanut butter on slices and top with raisins)
Thermos of hot chicken broth
Skim milk

Sandwich of cream cheese with mashed dates or alfalfa sprouts on raisin bread or bagel
Carrot and celery sticks
Hot coffee

Sandwich of sliced turkey and mashed avocado on pumpernickel bread (mashed avocado spread thickly on one slice of bread, topped with sliced turkey and a slice of buttered bread)
Dried apricots
Thermos of hot cider with cinnamon

Thermos of hearty bean and bacon soup
Sesame bread sticks
Pieces of raw broccoli sprinkled with lemon juice
Pear
Apple juice

Sandwich of sliced mushrooms and Swiss or Muenster cheese with mustard on cracked wheat bread
Sliced apple
Carton of milk

Container of antipasto salad: lettuce, tomato, chickpeas, olives, slices of salami or provolone cheese, with oil and vinegar dressing
Italian bread
Grapes
Iced coffee

Sandwich of apricot jam or dried apricots, chopped pecans, and cream cheese on whole wheat bread
Hot tea

Sandwich of corned beef with shredded red cabbage and mustard on a
   hard roll
Wedge of melon
Orange juice

Pumpernickel bread spread with cream cheese, topped with ham slices
   and crushed pineapple
Cherry tomatoes
Slice of watermelon
Iced coffee

French bread spread with blue cheese and topped with apple slices
Celery sticks
Plum
Mineral water with a wedge of lemon or lime

Thermos of onion topped with grated cheese
Wheat crackers
Dried apricots
Apple cider

Pita bread stuffed with a mixture of yogurt, sliced cucumbers, and black
   olives
Grapes
Hot tea with lemon

Sandwich of tuna salad with pickle relish on a bagel
Sunflower seeds
Tomato juice

Sandwich of sardine and egg salad (mashed sardines combined with
   chopped hard-boiled egg, mayonnaise, and a dash of lime juice) on
   pumpernickel bread
Cherry tomatoes
Banana
Vegetable juice

Sandwich of Muenster cheese, sliced tomatoes, and alfalfa sprouts with
   creamy Italian dressing on whole wheat bread
Pear
Mineral water with a wedge of lime

Raw green or red pepper strips, mushrooms, cauliflorets and carrot sticks
Container of creamy French dressing for dipping vegetables (1 cup of
   bottled dressing mixed with ½ cup of yogurt)
Thermos of beef soup
Bread sticks
Milk

Sandwich of bacon, cucumber slices, and bean sprouts with mayonnaise
on a hard roll
Pear
Milk

Cottage cheese mixed with diced red or green pepper and chopped chives
Slice of whole wheat brad
Celery and carrot sticks
Dates
Hot tea with lemon

Sandwich of chopped liver and diced onion with hard-boiled egg slices
on pumpernickel bread
Dill pickle
Tangerine
Hot coffee

Container of cubed avocado, shredded carrots and Swiss cheese, and
alfalfa sprouts with French dressing and a squeeze of lemon
Granola bar
Orange juice

Sandwich of sliced sausage or salami and roasted peppers with mustard
and lettuce on rye bread
Dried apricots with almonds
Grapefruit juice

Ricotta cheese mixed with raisins, apple slices, chopped walnuts, and a
sprinkling of cinnamon
Honey graham crackers
Grape juice

Pita bread stuffed with shredded cheddar cheese and tomato and zucchini
slices, mixed with a little mayonnaise and a dash of salt and pepper
Apple
Thermos of chicken broth

Sandwich of egg salad topped with alfalfa sprouts on whole wheat bread
Pickle spears
Chicken bouillon
Cranberry juice

Pita bread stuffed with chopped, steamed (or raw) broccoli spears, sliced
water chestnuts, sliced black olives, and a dash of Italian dressing
Granola bar
Mixed vegetable juice

Two hard-boiled eggs sliced lengthwise, spread with a mixture of olive
    pieces and mayonnaise, and put back together
Two celery sticks stuffed with farmer cheese
Seedless grapes
Lemonade

Container of crumbled tuna fish and chopped celery with a sprinkling of
    lemon juice
Kosher dill pickle
Banana
Ginger ale

Sandwich of pickled herring in sour cream, chopped parsley, and scal-
    lions on a lightly buttered hard roll
Tangerine
Gingersnaps
Iced tea

Container of carrot salad (1 cup of shredded carrots, ¼ cup of sour
    cream, and dashes of lemon juice and powdered ginger)
Bran muffin
Apple
Tomato juice

Sandwich of diced chicken and sliced water chestnuts (canned) with salt,
    pepper, and mayonnaise on a hard roll
Grapes
Cranberry juice

Container of garden salad (sliced zucchini, carrots, tomatoes, and cauli-
    florets) with creamy herb dressing (sour cream or yogurt mixed with
    fines herbes and a dash of lemon juice)
Jarlsberg cheese chunks
Matzo or other cracker
Pear
Pineapple-orange juice

Sandwich of cheese-scallion spread (½ cup of diced cheddar cheese, ½
    cup of cottage cheese, 1 tablespoon of mayonnaise, and 1 tablespoon
    of minced scallions) on rye bread
Peach
Iced tea with lemon

Thermos of cold fruit soup (1 cup of plain yogurt mixed with 1 cup of
    apricot nectar in a blender) with a liberal sprinkling of granola
Raisin bread
Iced coffee

Container of grapefruit sections, chunks of avocado, and grated cheddar
or Swiss cheese with citrus dressing (juice of 1 orange and 1 lemon,
¼ cup of salad oil, 1 teaspoon of honey, 1 teaspoon of sesame seeds,
and a dash of salt)
Fig bars
Iced tea with mint

Thermos of hot lentil soup
Celery sticks stuffed with cottage cheese and chives
Bran muffin
Cranberry juice

Potpourri salad (in a pint container, a 3-ounce can of drained tuna mixed
with slices of cucumber, green peas, chunks of cheddar cheese, and a
little Italian dressing)
Thermos of hot chicken consommé
Oatmeal cookie

Sandwich of cream cheese spread (a slice of whole wheat bread covered
with a layer of cream cheese, some finely chopped walnuts, diced
celery, and a sprinkle of cinnamon, and topped with another slice of
whole wheat bread)
Apple
Orange juice

Sandwich of pita bread and pepperoni (pita pocket stuffed with slices of
pepperoni, strips of green pepper, and some chopped onion)
Small can pineapple chunks
Iced tea

Sandwich of studded peanut butter (2 tablespoons of peanut butter
mixed with ½ cup of grated carrot) on raisin bread
Orange
Milk

Container of spinach dip (4 tablespoons of chopped fresh spinach mixed
with 1 cup of plain yogurt, ¼ teaspoon of garlic salt, and 2 table-
spoons of chopped onion)
Fresh vegetable sticks for dipping
Dried apricots
Herb tea

Sandwich of curried chicken salad (a 5-ounce can of chicken mixed with
2 tablespoons of mayonnaise and a hefty dash of curry powder) on
a hard roll
Kosher dill pickle
Wedge of favorite cheese
Ginger ale

Container of deli salad (diced Swiss cheese mixed with salami, celery, and hard-boiled egg, and Italian dressing to taste)
Bread sticks
Banana
Mineral water

Thermos of mushroom soup
Wedge of Gruyère cheese
Gingersnaps
Apple
Hot tea with lemon

Sandwich of Muenster cheese, alfalfa sprouts, and mustard on rye bread
Oatmeal cookies
Tomato juice

Container of tart fruit salad (one container of lemon yogurt mixed with a handful of raisins and ½ cup of canned pineapple chunks)
Graham crackers
Herb tea

Sandwich of bologna, American cheese, and well-drained sauerkraut on pumpernickel bread
Carrot sticks
Birch beer

Container of Mexican salad (½ head of shredded iceberg lettuce mixed with 1 cup of grated cheddar cheese, 1 chopped tomato, and mild taco sauce to taste)
Corn chips
Club soda with wedge of lime

Sandwich of sliced chicken and avocado with French dressing in a pita pocket
Dates
Vegetable juice

Container of Oriental salad (steamed snow peas, carrots, and cauliflorets mixed with teriyaki sauce to taste)
Granola bar
Orange juice

Sandwich of sliced turkey and cranberry sauce on whole wheat bread
Orange
Ginger ale

Container of carrot salad (1 cup of shredded carrots mixed with 2 tablespoons of raisins and 2 tablespoons of raspberry yogurt)
Bran muffin
Hot tea with lemon

Sandwich of meatloaf, Swiss cheese, and mayonnaise on whole wheat
bread
Tangerine
Club soda with wedge of lime

Container of turkey salad (1 cup of diced turkey mixed with chopped
apple half, diced celery stalk, and some mayonnaise)
Oatmeal cookie
Iced tea

Thermos of New England clam chowder
Raw broccoli spears
Corn muffin
Orange juice

Sandwich of cheddar cheese, sliced cucumbers, and French dressing on
pumpernickel bread
Small can of pears
Herb tea

Container of muchroom-zucchini salad (sliced mushrooms mixed with
raw zucchini slices, chopped scallions, and a little Italian dressing)
Sesame crackers
Banana
Hot coffee with cinnamon

Sandwich of crumbled tuna with sliced red onions and Russian dressing
on whole wheat bread
Green pepper rings
Dried apricots
Tomato juice

Container of robust salad (1 cup of shredded iceberg lettuce mixed with
marinated artichoke hearts, tomato wedges, and creamy herb dressing)
Stone wheat crackers
Apple
Ginger ale

Container of spinach salad (fresh spinach leaves mixed with diced
chicken, chopped almonds, and creamy herb dressing)
Potato chips
Pitted prunes

Container of fresh vegetable salad (broccoli florets, cherry tomatoes,
and chopped green olives tossed with oil and vinegar dressing)
Wheat crackers
Apple

Sandwich of salami, sliced sweet onion, green pepper strips, and mustard stuffed into a pita pocket
Kosher pickle
Peach
Peanut butter cookie

Sandwich of sliced ham, sweet pickle chips, and brown mustard on pumpernickel bread
Cherry tomatoes
Celery sticks
Oatmeal cookie

Sandwich of Muenster cheese, shredded carrots, and mayonnaise on whole wheat bread
Black olives
Orange

Sandwich of sliced turkey roll, Colby cheese, and bean sprouts on an onion roll
Sliced cucumbers
Cinnamon graham crackers

Container of sardine salad (1 can of sardines mixed with avocado slices and a squeeze of lemon juice)
Cauliflorets
Vanilla wafers

Container of plain yogurt mixed with sliced banana, flaked coconut, and a sprinkling of cinnamon
Celery sticks
Graham crackers
Iced tea

Sandwich of sliced avocado and chopped stuffed olives with mayonnaise in a pita pocket
Green pepper rings
Granola bar
Milk

Container of tuna salad (tuna mixed with chopped broccoli and tomatoes and bottled creamy herb dressing)
Melba toast
Date-nut bar
Ginger ale

Container of Chinese chicken salad (diced chicken mixed with chunks of canned pineapple and soy sauce)
Gingersnaps
Orange juice

Sandwich of liverwurst, thinly sliced red onion, and pickle relish with
mustard on pumpernickel
Raw green beans
Small can sliced peaches
Birch beer

Sandwich of cream cheese and apricot jam with chopped cashews on a
sliced bagel
Dill pickle spears
Oatmeal cookie
Cranberry juice

Sandwich of avocado slices and crumbled tuna with French dressing on
whole wheat bread
Carrot sticks
Oatmeal cookie
Hot coffee with cinnamon

Thermos of cream of mushroom soup
Sandwich of Muenster cheese, dill pickle chips, and mustard on pumper-
nickel bread
Apple
Ginger ale

Sandwich of turkey roll and tomato slices on buttered rye bread
Radishes
Peach
Club soda

Container of yogurt salad (1 cup of lemon yogurt mixed with mandarin
orange slices and sunflower seeds)
Date-nut bread
Tomato juice

Beef taco (slices of roast beef and Swiss cheese stuffed into a corn
tortilla)
Plum
Vegetable juice

Thermos of hot tomato soup
Container of Waldorf chicken salad (diced chicken and apples mixed with
some raisins and mayonnaise)
Celery sticks
Gingersnaps
Milk

Sandwich of Swiss cheese and sliced onion with brown mustard on rye bread
Dill pickle
Radishes
Oatmeal cookie

Container of mushroom salad (sliced mushrooms, slivered almonds, shredded Muenster or cheddar cheese, cherry tomatoes, and raisins tossed with Italian dressing)
Wheat crackers
Pear

Thermos of hot vegetable soup with a boiled hot dog (at lunchtime, shake out hot dog, stick it in a hot-dog bun, and drink soup)
Potato chips
Orange

Vegetable kabobs (cherry tomatoes, broccoli florets, and mushrooms skewered on a hibachi stick)
Corn chips
Coffee yogurt mixed with a handful of granola and chocolate chips

Container of Greek salad (½ head of shredded iceberg lettuce, crumbled feta cheese, chopped green pepper, and Greek olives tossed with oil and vinegar dressing)
Thermos of tomato soup
Oyster crackers
Brownie

Sandwich of corned beef and sauerkraut on an onion roll
Black olives
Applesauce

Sandwich of chicken salad (chunks of chicken mixed with bacon bits, mayonnaise, and a dab of Dijon mustard) on white bread
Raw string beans
Apple

Sandwich of cream cheese, sliced cucumbers, and a pinch of dill on a pumpernickel bagel
Carrot sticks
Tangerine

Container of green bean salad (raw string beans, sliced mushrooms, and chopped scallions tossed with French dressing)
Corn muffin
Tangerine

Sandwich of canned salmon mixed with sliced olives and mayonnaise on whole wheat bread
Green pepper rings
Chocolate chip cookie

Sandwich of zucchini rounds and Swiss cheese with Russian dressing on rye bread
Potato chips
Pear

Thermos of chili
Soda crackers
Carrot sticks
Orange

Container of spinach salad (fresh spinach, sliced pepperoni, and cheddar cheese cubes tossed with Italian dressing)
Bread sticks
Canned peaches

Thermos of navy bean soup
Sandwich of sliced chicken and a canned pineapple ring on white bread
Cauliflorets
Brownie

Sandwich of alfalfa sprouts and sliced Colby cheese with mayonnaise on onion roll
Celery sticks
Granola bar

Thermos of chicken noodle soup
Gingersnaps spread with cream cheese
Broccoli florets
Apple

Container of plain yogurt mixed with sliced bananas and canned mandarin orange segments
Whole wheat crackers
Green pepper rings
Granola bar

Container of flavorful salad (marinated artichoke hearts, bacon bits, and shredded iceberg lettuce mixed with French dressing)
Sesame crackers
Dried apricots

Sandwich of whipped cream cheese, sliced stuffed olives, and cucumber rounds on an onion roll
Corn chips
Pear

Sandwich of sliced salami, mozzarella cheese, and dark mustard on a
  hard roll
Kosher dill pickle
Brownie

Container of tuna salad (zucchini rounds, cherry tomatoes, and tuna
  mixed with Italian dressing)
Potato chips
Apple

Sandwich of curried egg salad (two diced hard-boiled eggs mixed with
  mayonnaise, curry powder, and chopped red pepper) on pumpernickel bread
Sweet pickle chips
Canned peaches

Sandwich of liverwurst and horseradish on rye bread
Broccoli florets
Applesauce with a dash of cinnamon

Sandwich of sliced turkey and apple butter on whole wheat bread
Celery sticks
Chocolate chip cookie

LOW-CALORIE LUNCHES TO TAKE TO WORK

Finding a low-calorie, low-cost lunch is a real problem if you're a desk-bound dieter, especially if you order your meal from a local coffee shop. So why not bring along the diet delicacies you'd make for yourself if you weren't working?

Here are menus (all well under 400 calories) and recipes for a week's worth of tempting lunchbox specials; among them are: cold chicken and vegetables with thyme, a tomato stuffed with cottage cheese salad, and a spicy low-calorie gazpacho combined with water-packed tuna. A helpful hint: Keeping colorful paper goods, plastic utensils, a can opener, and a mug in the office will make lunch so pleasant you may forget you're on a diet.

MONDAY	
HOT TOMATO JUICE (½ cup)	25
ASSORTED RAW VEGETABLES AND	
HARD-BOILED EGG	140
YOGURT FOR DIPPING	65
WEDGE OF CANTALOUPE	15
	245

VEGETABLES WITH YOGURT DIP

    8 carrot sticks or curls (see Note)
    6 celery sticks (1 stalk celery)
    6 (½ small) zucchini or cucumber sticks, pared
    5 cauliflorets
    2 radishes
       Cherry tomatoes or whole tomato
    ½ cup yogurt
    2 tablespoons finely snipped chives or watercress or dill

Place vegetables in a bowl of ice until ready to use. Drain and pack in plastic bag.

Combine yogurt with chives.

To serve: Dip vegetables in yogurt.

Notes: To make carrot curls, make thin strips full length of carrot with a vegetable parer. Curl up and fasten with a wooden pick. Chill.

To hard-boil eggs: Cover eggs with water to an inch above them; bring rapidly to a boil. Take pan off heat; cover and let stand for 20 minutes. Cool eggs immediately in cold water, to prevent dark surface on yolks and to remove shells easily.

TUESDAY	
HOT CONSOMMÉ (1 cup)	53
TOMATO FILLED WITH	
COTTAGE CHEESE SALAD	135
MELBA TOAST	20
SMALL FRESH PEAR	55
	263

HOT CONSOMMÉ

½ can (10½-oz size) condensed beef consommé
1 tablespoon sliced green onion

In a small saucepan, combine consommé and ½ cup of water. Bring to a boil. Add green onion. Remove from heat. Pour into vacuum bottle to keep hot.
Makes 1 cup (1 serving).

TOMATO FILLED WITH COTTAGE CHEESE SALAD

1 medium tomato
½ cup diet creamed cottage cheese
4 teaspoons grated pared carrot
4 teaspoons diced green pepper
4 teaspoons finely chopped green onion

Cut ½-inch-thick slice from stem end of each tomato. With a spoon, scoop out pulp and seeds; chop pulp. Drain tomatoes.
In a small bowl, mix cottage cheese, carrot, green pepper, green onion, and chopped tomato pulp; mix lightly. Spoon into tomato.
Makes 1 cup (1 serving).

WEDNESDAY

GAZPACHO WITH TUNA	206
UNSALTED CRACKERS (2)	26
HOT TEA	0
	232

GAZPACHO WITH TUNA

1 medium green pepper
1 medium cucumber
1 small onion, peeled
1 teaspoon salt
  Dash of dried basil leaves
1 tablespoon red wine vinegar
1 can (18-oz size) tomato juice, chilled
1 medium tomato, peeled
1 can (3½-oz size) water-packed tuna

In an electric blender, combine half of green pepper, cubed; half of peeled and cubed cucumber; half of onion, quartered; salt; basil; red wine vinegar; and ½ cup of tomato juice.

Blend mixture, covered, at high speed for 30 seconds to puree vegetables.

Stir in remaining tomato juice. Pour half into a vacuum jug. Store remainder of gazpacho in refrigerator for another time.

Chop separately remaining green pepper, cucumber, onion, and tomato. Use half with gazpacho. Store other half in plastic wrap in refrigerator.

At serving time, drain tuna and add to gazpacho. Sprinkle with chopped vegetables.

Makes 2 servings.

THURSDAY

EGG AND TOMATO ACCORDION	189
ITALIAN BREAD STICKS (2)	40
BUNCH OF GREEN GRAPES (½ cup)	35
HOT TEA WITH LEMON	2
	266

EGG AND TOMATO ACCORDION

- 1 medium tomato
- 1 hard-boiled egg
- 3 tablespoons low-calorie mayonnaise
- 2 teaspoons catsup
- ¼ teaspoon dried dillweed

Cut tomato into 8 slices, ¼ inch apart, accordion style (don't cut all the way through); spread apart slightly.

Cut egg into 7 slices. In a small bowl, combine mayonnaise, catsup, and dillweed.

Spoon 1 teaspoon of mayonnaise mixture between each 2 tomato slices. Gently put a slice of egg between each 2 tomato slices. Push wooden pick through tomato to keep shape. Wrap in foil or plastic wrap and refrigerate.

Makes 1 serving.

FRIDAY	
COLD BREAST OF CHICKEN	250
TOMATOES AND CUCUMBER WITH	
YOGURT DRESSING	60
HOT TEA	0
	310

COLD BREAST OF CHICKEN

1 small onion, sliced
1 celery stalk, sliced
1 carrot, pared and sliced
1 parsley sprig
¼ teaspoon salt
⅛ teaspoon dried thyme leaves
1 chicken bouillon cube
3 whole black peppers
One 12-oz whole chicken breast, split

In a large skillet, combine onion, celery, carrot, parsley, salt, thyme, bouillon cube, black peppers, 2 cups of water, and chicken breast. Bring mixture to a boil.

Reduce heat and simmer, covered, for 30 minutes, or just until chicken breast is fork-tender.

Remove from heat. Let chicken cool in broth; refrigerate until chilled.

Remove chicken breast from broth; reserve broth. Remove skin from chicken breast. Spoon ¼ cup of broth and vegetables over each chicken breast. Pack in plastic box with lid for carrying.

Makes 2 servings.

TOMATOES AND CUCUMBERS WITH YOGURT DRESSING

Dressing:
¾ cup yogurt
4 teaspoons chopped mint leaves

½ cucumber, pared and sliced
6 cherry tomatoes

Combine yogurt and mint leaves. Mix well and refrigerate. Use about 3 tablespoons of dressing for cucumber and tomatoes.

Makes ¾ cup.

SOME THOUGHTS ON STUDENT LUNCHES

"I'll trade you a peanut butter for your tuna fish."

"Nah, take it. I'm just gonna drink my juice and go outside."

Similar conversations take place in lunchrooms across the country. Mothers groan to hear them. It's hard enough for a working parent to find the time to prepare nutritious and appealing lunches day after day without having to worry that the food children carry may not end up in their tummies.

The ideas and tips that follow, many gathered from working moms, should help make your lunches surefire successes—and also make it easier for you to face the daily lunchbox routine.

First off, give some thought to your child's lunch period. Grade-school lunchtime is often short, and children want to play and socialize as well as eat. When the lunches are brought out at nursery school, some kids are too wound up to eat, while others feel more like napping.

One nursery school teacher says the biggest mistake most parents make is in overestimating how much their children can eat. Sending along many different foods in little containers is also inappropriate. Most small children find it overwhelming to mix and match a "buffet" lunch, and there's often not enough time or incentive to do it. Intense peer pressure around the lunch table can interfere with what is eaten, too. Kids are as concerned that their lunches be "in" as that they include favorite foods. While first grader Lisa loves deviled eggs at family picnics, she told her mother that they're too weird for school lunches.

Lunch-swapping is very popular with elementary schoolchildren. It's easiest to acknowledge this and work from there. Perhaps you can find out what your child is receiving in return for his or her lunch, and pack that item. Or provide some extras meant especially for trading— a half sandwich or a few more cookies.

Encourage your children to take over some of the planning and preparing of their lunches. Their imaginations can turn the humdrum activity of lunch-making into fun. Food that children have chosen themselves is more likely to get eaten, and in the process lots can be learned about making decisions, handling food, and balancing meals nutritionally.

Even preschoolers can help make and pack lunches. Tearing lettuce for sandwiches, mixing up egg salad, or putting snacks in plastic bags are just some of the simple chores they can handle.

A Note About Nutrition

Lunch should supply about one-third of a child's daily nutritional requirements and caloric needs. That translates into one serving of milk or an equivalent dairy product, one serving of a protein-rich food, one serving of bread or another cereal or grain product, and one serving of a fruit or vegetable.

There's more leeway in this plan than meets the eye. For example, the protein portion of the meal could be meat ravioli or a mashed garbanzo bean spread, as well as the traditional peanut butter, tuna, bologna, or ham and cheese. A container of yogurt or a chunk of cheese can be substituted for the milk; crackers, muffins, or rice can stand in for the bread.

Sandwiches

Sandwiches are the overwhelming favorite of the school lunch bunch, and the winners are peanut butter, cold cuts and luncheon meats, cheese, and tuna and egg salad. But there's no reason you can't experiment now and then to add variety to the lunchbox. These ideas will help spur your creativity.

• Since children love crunchy textures, try adding crisp vegetables to sandwiches. Chopped green or red pepper, shredded carrots and cabbage, zucchini slices, bean sprouts, and drained sauerkraut can all be mixed into or layered with fillings between the bread. Juicier vegetables, such as tomato and cucumber slices and pickles, should be packed separately to keep the bread from getting soggy.

• Kids' fondness for salty foods can be satisfied by blending some pickle relish, chopped olives, or chopped peanuts into sandwich fillings.

• For those with a sweet tooth, combine chopped dried apricots or prunes, raisins, chopped apples, diced peeled oranges, sliced bananas, shredded coconut, or grated orange peel with cream cheese, cottage cheese, peanut butter, or tuna salad.

• Sunflower seeds, chopped almonds, sesame seeds, and wheat germ add protein and crunch to sandwich fillings.

• To extend tuna or egg salad, bind it with cottage cheese instead of mayonnaise. And if you can sneak them in, cubes of tofu (soybean curd) are an inexpensive way to boost the protein of salad mixtures.

• Substitute shredded cheese for the more traditional sliced cheese in sandwiches. Blend together a variety—cheddar, Muenster, and Swiss, for example.

• A mother I know tried two variations on the peanut-butter-and-jelly theme, both to the liking of her fussy five-year-old: A blend of peanut butter and applesauce creates a lighter spread; peanut butter mixed with honey and unsweetened cocoa makes for a sandwich that tastes like chocolate bars.

• According to Stephen, a seasoned lunch carrier, "Pita sandwiches are the best because the guts don't come out." Pita bread is a nice holder for salads mixed with mayonnaise or dressing. Before filling, line the inside of the pocket with lettuce leaves or slices of cheese.

• To convert seven-year-old Erica from a white-bread diet, her mom creates sandwiches using a slice of whole wheat bread and a slice of white. She then cuts the sandwich into quarters and turns over two of the pieces to make a checkerboard design.

• For variety, make sandwiches with taco shells, muffins, bagels, or crackers instead of bread. The toddler and nursery school set might appreciate mini-sandwiches made on tiny bagels or cocktail pumpernickel or rye bread. Homemade quick breads such as banana, pumpkin, and date-nut are sweet alternatives to store-bought bread. When time permits, bake a few loaves and freeze in slices that can be made into sandwiches quickly. They're wonderful spread with cream cheese, peanut butter, and semisoft cheeses.

• After four-year-old Stephen rearranged his cheese sandwich, his mother began preparing "inside-out sandwiches" all the time. To duplicate Stephen's creation, put the cheese slices on the outside and the bread slice in the middle; wrap in foil or plastic film to hold.

• When Richard, a teenager now, was little, he loved his mom's idea of using apple slices for sandwich covers instead of bread. She used to spread large apple slices with peanut butter or semisoft cheese and then press two slices together to make a sandwich.

• Another alternative to the traditional sandwich is to roll up the filling in large romaine leaves or spread it on celery stalks. You might also try threading chunks of meat, cubes of cheese, cherry tomatoes, and other vegetable or fruit pieces on bamboo skewers for a kabob lunch.

Tummy Warmers

On a blustery day, most children would welcome something warm to eat at lunchtime. Widemouthed Thermoses are especially handy for toting soups, stews, and other hot foods. Here are some suggestions for filling these containers.

• Leftover homemade soup or canned condensed soup makes a luscious lunch. Pack along popcorn or little crackers to float on top.

• Milk-based soups are ideal for children who don't like to drink plain milk. Add bits of cooked meat or poultry or leftover cooked vegetables to make the soup extra chunky. Hot cocoa is an almost foolproof way to get milk into kids.

• Chili, macaroni and cheese, and franks and beans all travel well to school.

• Cooked corn on the cob fits perfectly into a widemouthed vacuum bottle.

Packing in Some Fun

If a child is feeling lonely or cranky at noon, even the most terrific lunch won't entice her to eat. But a "little something extra" packed along with the meal might cheer her up and whet her appetite. Here are some ideas for ways to make lunchtime special for your child.

• For a once-in-a-while surprise, wrap a sandwich in colorful gift wrap and tie with a ribbon. (Be sure to cover the sandwich with foil or plastic wrap first.)

• Cut sandwiches into different shapes with a cookie cutter or a knife. For a preschooler who is learning to identify shapes, you might cut a sandwich into triangles, diamonds, squares, and so forth.

• Younger children delight in garnishes. Carrot curls, radish slices, zucchini rounds, olives, and cherry tomatoes, as well as grapes, pineapple chunks, and dried apricots can be speared with toothpicks and attached to sandwiches.

• Turn lunchtime into party time for your preschooler by sending along an assortment of finger foods for him to share with his friends. Try those small cubes of cheese wrapped in foil, little boxes of raisins, and sesame bread sticks.

• Berries, grapes, and dried fruits can be packed along with vanilla or fruit-flavored yogurt for a dipping snack.

• Cut-up raw vegetables are also fun to eat with a dip. For a change of pace from carrot and celery sticks, try florets of broccoli and cauliflower, rings of green and sweet red pepper, zucchini and summer squash sticks, cherry tomatoes, peas in the pod, and trimmed green beans. The dip can be as simple as plain yogurt mixed with seasoned salt. Pack it in a plastic margarine container that can be discarded.

• Make up a big batch of "munch mix" to keep on hand—it stores indefinitely when sealed tightly. Include small shredded wheat biscuits, popcorn, dried fruit, raisins, soybeans, sunflower seeds, animal crackers, and peanut M&Ms. Even the smallest child can help put this mix together and pack it in individual sandwich bags.

• When time permits, bake up some lunchbox goodies with your kids. Cookies, muffins, and quick breads can all be made ahead and frozen.

• A fruity milkshake is a great change from juice or plain milk: Simply whirl milk and a banana, berries, or other fresh or canned fruit in the blender and pour into a Thermos.

• Homemade applesauce (especially if it's cooked with the help of your child) is sure to be a hit. Pack in a small plastic container and include a spoon.

• One nursery school teacher reports that several moms please their preschoolers by writing out a simple menu listing the contents of the lunchbox. Beginning readers might be able to pick out the words by themselves, and others can have a teacher read their menus to them.

• As a change from plain white paper goods, pack napkins or paper plates left over from your child's birthday party. They'll bring back happy memories at lunchtime.

• Have your child decorate some brown-paper lunch bags with crayon drawings, stickers, and other colorful items.

• Save the foil trays from TV dinners to use for lunch-packing. Place a sandwich in one compartment, fruit in another, and a special treat in the third. Overwrap tray securely with foil.

• Pack some moistened towelettes in foil packets. If your child finds them more fun to use than napkins, maybe he will.

• Tuck a little note in with your child's lunch. One as simple as "See you soon. Love, Mom" shows a child that you care.

Time-Saving Tips

To avoid the morning lunch-packing crunch, many families find it helpful to do some preparation ahead. Here are some suggestions.

• Group all lunch fixings in one section of the refrigerator and label them, if necessary. That way, beverages, fruits, cut-up vegetables, sandwich fillings, and bread will be handy when you want them.

• Make one or two weeks' worth of sandwiches at a time and freeze them. Wrapped airtight, sandwiches can be kept in the freezer for two weeks. (Packed into a lunchbox, a frozen sandwich will thaw by lunchtime.) Fillings that freeze well include peanut butter, cheese spread, cooked chicken or turkey, ham, bologna, and other luncheon meats. Avoid freezing sandwiches made with mayonnaise. And leave out jelly and fresh vegetables.

Set up a sandwich-making assembly line. Arrange bread slices two by two in rows. Then set up filling ingredients and condiments. One family member can spread the bread with butter or margarine, another can do the filling, and a third can add the second slice of bread, cut the sandwich in half, and wrap it.

Playing It Safe

Since school lunches are often kept at room temperature for several hours, they provide the perfect breeding ground for the type of bacteria that cause food poisoning. But packed lunches will remain safe from spoilage if you follow three basic rules: Keep cold foods cold, keep hot foods hot, and keep all food clean.

Keeping food clean means making sure your hands and any equipment that touches the food are washed first with soap and water. It's important to keep kitchen counters and cutting boards as spotless as possible—transfer of germs is common on these surfaces, especially if they've been in contact with raw meat. The cleanliness rule should extend to any lunch-carrying containers too. Always wash lunchboxes, vacuum bottles, and plastic containers after each use.

Keeping cold foods cold and hot foods hot is not too difficult, even if there's no refrigerator or heating device around. As mentioned before, vacuum containers and insulated bottles are available in many sizes, and they'll keep food at the correct temperature for several hours. If a container is going to hold cold food, chill it first with ice water; pour boiling water into the container to heat it before filling with hot food.

You can buy liquid and gel freezer packs in your supermarket. They can be frozen and then popped into your child's lunchbox or bag in the morning to keep food cold until lunchtime.

One last warning: No sandwich of any kind should be stored on top of a classroom radiator. The heat will cause harmful bacteria to multiply in no time.

CHAPTER SEVEN
AFTER-SCHOOL SNACKS

When the school bell rings, most kids hurry home and head straight for the refrigerator. Even though you probably can't be home to personally supervise the snack, you can make sure that the food on hand is appealing and nutritious. We asked a group of kids what food they like to have waiting for them after a hard day in the classroom. We discovered that kids are pretty adaptable and will settle for yogurt if there aren't any cookies in the cupboard. Not surprisingly, we found that although children are a resourceful lot—able to whip up a snack during a single commercial—they are conservative, preferring predictability over variety.

Scott, for instance, is already firmly set in his ways at the ripe old age of five and a half. He insists on a bologna sandwich with American cheese every single day. His mother's job is to make sure the ingredients are available so the sitter can fix the sandwich for Scott.

Seven-year-old Benjamin, like many of his contemporaries, is not crazy about the food served in the school cafeteria, so he's starved by the time he gets home at three o'clock. He favors a snack that could be mistaken for a second lunch: a couple of traditional peanut butter and jelly sandwiches, which he makes for himself, generally followed by an orange or apple.

For five-year-old Cecily, a p. b. and j. sandwich is completely out of the question. She prefers a dish of vanilla or strawberry ice cream.

Erica, age ten, says she looks forward to the days when her mother has baked for a party because she then makes Erica's favorite snack: graham crackers smothered with chocolate buttercream frosting. On ordinary afternoons, Erica helps herself to wheat crackers that, depending on her mood, she sometimes tops with cheddar cheese. She reports that her seven-year-old brother Robby's favorite snack is a bowl of cereal with milk, a choice Erica finds "disgusting" for that time of day.

A self-proclaimed cookie monster at age nine, Adam thrives on chocolate chip cookies dipped in peanut butter. He washes this feast down with a glass of cold milk.

Like Adam, Kimberly, age eleven, has an active sweet tooth. She confesses that she usually picks up a candy bar on the way home from school and likes just a glass of chocolate milk when she gets home. Once in a while she munches on a few carrot sticks while she is doing her homework.

Not all kids are as hooked on sweets as Kimberly. Six-year-old Kevin, for example, enjoys the tuna salad his mother leaves for him in a bowl in the refrigerator.

Lisa, at age six, also possesses a prosaic palate. When her mother is home to make them, Lisa snacks on toasted cheese sandwiches; otherwise she'll have some plain yogurt with honey.

Eight-year-old Sarah, on the other hand, is more flexible: "I like just about everything my mother has left over." Sarah does admit to a weakness for the egg salad her mother often leaves for her in the refrigerator.

Displaying the inventiveness of a chef or scientist, Melissa, age nine, enjoys cooking up a batch of popcorn. Then she munches on it while she watches TV or reads a book.

Another eight-year-old, Rachel, is content to share a container of plain yogurt with her sister. Sometimes, when Rachel is really hungry, she'll add some raisins or dried apricots.

A fellow devotee of plain yogurt, ten-year-old Greg admits that he occasionally likes an Oreo cookie, but insists he never eats more than two at one sitting.

Some kids, like ten-year-old Sasha, thrive on variety. He lists a few of his favorite after-school treats: doughnuts, cake, and potato chips. He likes to accompany his goodies with a tall glass of orange juice.

Their tastes are as diverse as the kids themselves. But one thing they all have in common is the amazing capacity to wolf down their delicious concoctions and still eat a big dinner three hours later!

Here are more suggestions that may tempt them. You probably have most of the ingredients in the house. If not, the children can use their imagination to make substitutions. Some require a little preparation the night before—like boiling eggs and peeling vegetables—but when it's snacktime, they're easy to put together. The snacks that require cooking are for children old enough to use the stove or toaster oven. Post these suggestions on the refrigerator door. The rest is up to the kids.

Oatmeal cookies spread with cream cheese make a nice change and go well with orange sections.

Tangerine sections (or slices of any other fresh fruit) mixed with plain yogurt or sour cream with a sprinkle of cinnamon on top. Honey can be used as a sweetener.

Applesauce spread on graham crackers, along with a tall glass of cold milk.

Celery, radishes, cauliflower, and carrots cut up and kept in a container of ice water in the refrigerator. Keep a package of onion soup mix on hand to combine with sour cream or plain yogurt. It's a great vegetable dip.

Banana shake: Put one cup of milk, one sliced banana, and one raw egg in a blender and mix well. Malted milk powder can also be added.

A mixture of raisins, cashews, and any other nuts or sunflower seeds. Dried apricots can also be added.

Deviled eggs: Slice hard-boiled eggs lengthwise; remove yolks and mix with cottage cheese or mayonnaise and relish. Replace mixture in the whites.

Tuna fish salad made with a can of tuna, mayonnaise, seedless grapes, and chopped walnuts. Spread mixture on crackers and sprinkle alfalfa sprouts on top.

Pita bread slit and stuffed with crumbled hard-boiled eggs, a few dabs of mayonnaise, and some shredded lettuce. For adventurous children, add canned anchovies.

Tomato juice with a dash of Worcestershire sauce and a squeeze of lemon as an accompaniment to crackers and sliced cheddar cheese.

A dill pickle wrapped in a slice of American cheese—or two dill pickles wrapped in two slices of American cheese—will give a child enough energy to set the table, do his or her homework, and go out to play.

A fresh-fruit combination of strawberries, sliced peaches, and bananas. Add a little orange juice to the compote for a tart flavor.

Spread toast with tuna fish salad and top with a slice of American cheese. Put under broiler until cheese is melted.

Cinnamon toast and potluck fruit punch: Butter some toast and sprinkle with a combination of sugar and cinnamon. To make punch, combine whatever fruit juices are on hand (such as lemonade, orange juice, and apple juice) and add a slice of orange and a strawberry.

Cover vegetables in sour cream: Combine slices of scallions, string beans, radishes, tomatoes, and cucumbers with sour cream and a dash of salt.

Frozen juice pops: Fill molds (they are available at supermarkets and discount stores) with fruit juice (or even chocolate milk) and freeze.

Granola, nuts, and raisins combined in a container of plain yogurt. A child with an incurable sweet tooth could add some honey.

Date-nut bread spread with cream cheese and dotted with walnuts and orange sections.

Bread sticks lightly dipped in mustard or mayonnaise, accompanied by chunks of Jarlsberg or Muenster cheese.

Spread graham crackers with farmer cheese and orange marmalade. Drink a mug of hot cocoa with this combination.

Combine cottage cheese with applesauce and mashed banana; top with sunflower seeds and a sprinkling of nutmeg.

Cover half a toasted English muffin with tomato sauce, top with slices of mozzarella cheese, and sprinkle with chopped green pepper. Broil muffin (on aluminum foil to avoid a mess) in a toaster-oven until cheese melts.

Put canned peaches or plums in a saucepan over low heat and sprinkle with cinnamon. When nice and hot, transfer to a bowl, add a dollop of sour cream, and eat!

Fill up with a yogurt shake! Put 1 cup of orange juice, ½ container of yogurt, 1 tablespoon of honey, and a sliced banana in a blender. Mix well.

Cinnamon toast eaten with a peeled orange is a great snack. To make the topping for buttered toast, mix 1 teaspoon of sugar and a dash of cinnamon.

Dip carrot and celery strips in chunky peanut butter or soft cheddar cheese.

Liven up plain yogurt with chunks of apple and a tablespoon of breakfast cereal. Top with a little brown sugar.

To make a quick cranberry-banana slush, slice 2 large bananas into a blender. Add 1 can (6-oz size) of frozen cranberry drink (unthawed) and mix until well blended. Pour into parfait glasses and eat with a spoon or drink with a straw. This recipe makes enough to share with a friend.

Split and toast an English muffin. Mix together 2 tablespoons of farmer cheese and 1 tablespoon of strawberry jam. Divide cheese mixture and spread over muffin halves. Top with nuts or raisins.

Chop together a hard-boiled egg and some iceberg lettuce. Add enough French dressing or mayonnaise to make everything hold together. Spread mixture on two slices of whole wheat bread and cut each slice into four pieces. Top with a little pickle relish or olives.

For a handy snack bowl, gently remove one whole leaf of iceberg lettuce from the head. Fill with grapes, apple slices, nuts, and dried fruits. Carry it out to play; when you finish the snack you can eat the lettuce bowl. You don't have to remember to bring home the dish or hunt for a trash can to throw away a paper container.

Toast a tortilla and spread with your favorite bean or onion dip, or flavored cheese spread. Top with chopped lettuce and some sliced dill pickles or olives. If you don't have a tortilla, use a pita or a piece of toast.

Toast a frozen whole wheat waffle, butter it, and top with apple slices, or drained canned peach slices, and honey.

Mix a chilled can of rice pudding with some fresh orange slices or canned mandarin orange sections, drained. Spooned into a parfait glass, the pudding looks as good as it tastes!

Fill a hot dog bun or small French bread with shredded cheese, cabbage, lettuce, and carrots. Top with a tomato slice and some oil and vinegar dressing for a submarine sandwich.

For a peanut butter milk shake, measure 1½ cups of milk, ¼ cup of smooth peanut butter, and 1 tablespoon of honey into a blender. Mix until smooth.

Wash a medium tomato. Cut out core and place tomato cut-end up on a salad plate. Make cuts almost to bottom, dividing tomato into 6 wedges. Gently spread wedges open to make a flower. Fill center with plain or vegetable cottage cheese (or leftover egg salad or coleslaw).

Spread a slice of bologna with mustard or cheese spread and wrap around a sesame bread stick.

Make your own yogurt or cottage cheese sundaes: Place a scoop of your favorite thick yogurt or cottage cheese in a bowl and top with fruit and granola, unprocessed bran, wheat germ, or Grapenuts.

In a dish, blend 2 tablespoons of peanut butter with 1 tablespoon of honey. Toast a frozen waffle, spread with peanut butter-honey mixture, and top with a few dried apricots.

Mix 2 tablespoons of whipped cream cheese with 1 teaspoon of raisins and 1 teaspoon of unsalted peanuts or soybeans. Toast a corn muffin or toaster cake and spread with cheese mixture.

Crumble several graham crackers into a bowl. Add 2 heaping spoonfuls of plain or vanilla yogurt. Stir. Top with a few green grapes.

Split and toast a whole wheat English muffin. Top with cheddar cheese spread. Press some apple slices into cheese and enjoy!

Pour 1 cup of cold milk into a blender. Add a small can of vanilla pudding and ½ cup of blueberries. Blend until smooth. Put in a tall glass and drink.

Warm a tortilla in toaster-oven for a minute or so, then stuff softened tortilla with sticks of Monterey Jack cheese. Spoon some prepared taco sauce over cheese, if you like extra zip.

Sprinkle 1 tablespoon of flaked coconut onto a sheet of waxed paper.

Over a sink, drizzle 1 tablespoon of honey onto a banana, twirling banana to coat all sides. Roll banana in coconut.

Wrap a hot dog in a slice of American cheese and then in an unbaked refrigerator biscuit. Secure with a wooden toothpick. Heat on a piece of foil in toaster-oven for several minutes, or until biscuit turns golden. Dip in mustard.

Mix 1 teaspoon of sweet pickle relish with 1 tablespoon of mayonnaise. Halve a hard-boiled egg and dip into flavored mayonnaise.

Put two canned peach halves in a bowl. Top with a generous dollop of sour cream. Sprinkle on a bit of brown sugar or cinnamon-sugar.

Empty half a can of undiluted cheese soup into a foil pie plate. Stir in 1 tablespoon of water, a dash of Worcestershire sauce, and a little mustard. Heat in toaster-oven until warm and smooth. Dip bread sticks into mixture.

Stuff a pita with some alfalfa sprouts. Tuck in a couple of small carrot sticks and strips of green pepper. Spoon in 2 tablespoons of cottage cheese and 1 teaspoon of Thousand Island salad dressing.

Spread some deviled ham on a slice of toasted pumpernickel bread. Press a few dill or sweet pickle slices into ham.

Spread 2 wheat crackers with peanut butter. Put a slice of cucumber on each cracker and press together to form a sandwich.

Wash a pear or an apple. Slice in half through core. Use a grapefruit spoon or measuring teaspoon to scoop out core. Fill space where core was and spread cut surface with cheddar cheese spread or peanut butter. Put halves back together.

Layer 3 graham crackers (or oatmeal-raisin cookies) with orange marmalade and cottage cheese.

Warm some cider. Add a cinnamon stick and drink along with a piece of rye bread spread with butter and plum jam.

Mix equal parts of club soda and Cranapple juice and add some ice.

Carefully wash a cucumber or carrot. Peel and cut cucumber lengthwise into quarters or trim ends from carrot. Wrap a slice of Swiss cheese or Muenster cheese around cucumber quarter or carrot and fasten with a toothpick. Other cheeses may be used if they will roll without breaking.

Mix 1 tablespoon of whipped cream cheese with 1 teaspoon of strawberry preserves. Spread mixture on a slice of whole wheat bread and sprinkle with a little wheat germ.

For a quick fruit cobbler, open a small can of sliced peaches and pour into a bowl. Sprinkle with cinnamon and granola, and top with yogurt or vanilla ice cream.

Make a bread pizza by slicing a hero roll in half lengthwise. Toast halves lightly in toaster-oven. Spoon some prepared spaghetti sauce on each half and top with slices of mozzarella cheese. Heat in toaster-oven again until cheese melts.

Mix half a small can of tuna with a spoonful of mayonnaise and a little horseradish. Cut a green pepper in half, remove seeds and membranes, and stuff halves with tuna mixture.

Split a whole wheat pita. Open a small can of fruit cocktail and drain. Mix fruit in a bowl with 2 tablespoons of cottage cheese and 1 tablespoon of whole or slivered almonds. Spoon fruit mixture into pita.

Split a bagel and toast both halves. While bagel halves are hot, spread with cream cheese. Place a pineapple ring on top of one half, press several walnut halves into the other, and put together to make a sandwich.

Combine bite-size pieces of leftover chicken or turkey with golden raisins, almonds, and a little mayonnaise. Stuff mixture into a pita pocket.

Split a bran muffin in half. Butter and top each half with a spoonful of applesauce and a dash of cinnamon. Put two halves together or eat as an open-face sandwich.

Slice a hard-boiled egg and put into a pita pocket along with a little mayonnaise and some shredded lettuce. Add a sprinkling of bacon bits.

Toast a frozen waffle. Spread with cream cheese and top with some fresh orange segments.

Split and toast a bagel. Spread each half with a little mustard and top with a slice of salami and several avocado slices.

Open and drain a small can of pineapple chunks; turn into a bowl. Add several large spoonfuls of vanilla yogurt and stir. Eat with crackers or a granola bar.

Toast a slice of whole wheat bread. Spread with butter. Top with a few dried apricot slices or some coconut flakes.

Put a chicken bouillon cube into a mug. Carefully add boiling water and stir until cube is dissolved. Break an egg into a bowl and beat with a fork. Pour egg into hot broth and stir. Eat with carrot or bread sticks.

Mix ½ cup of mayonnaise with a pinch of curry powder. Use as a dip with radishes and string beans.

Wash a pear. Slice in half and scoop out core with a teaspoon. Put a large dollop of cottage cheese on each half and top with a little French dressing.

Put 1 cup of milk, 1 sliced banana, 1 teaspoon of smooth peanut butter, and a dash of nutmeg into a blender. Whirl for 30 seconds to make a banana-nut shake.

Place some ham and tomato slices on a tortilla and roll it up. Dip in taco sauce.

Spread graham crackers with apple butter and sprinkle with sunflower seeds. Eat with a glass of cold milk.

Combine 2 tablespoons of sour cream and a dash each of catsup and onion powder. Use as a dip for raw vegetables such as carrot and celery sticks and broccoli florets.

Empty a can of mandarin orange slices into a blender. Add a cup of cranberry juice and mix for 30 seconds.

Stuff celery stalks with cream cheese and sprinkle lightly with paprika.

Heat a can of condensed tomato soup in a saucepan with 1 can of water and 2 tablespoons of Parmesan cheese. Eat with whole wheat bread sticks.

Open an individual container of prepared rice pudding. Top with some raisins and chopped nuts, and stir.

APPENDIXES:
PREPARATION AND STORAGE TIPS

Appendix I
THE TIME MACHINES: KITCHEN APPLIANCES THAT CUT CORNERS

Nobody ever seems to have enough time for everything, but working mothers have less time than anybody. A goodly portion of that time, especially on weekday evenings, is likely to be spent in the kitchen, which is why kitchen appliances are one of the best investments a working mother can make.

When you're considering an appliance, your best guide is your own work pattern. How long do you spend in the kitchen now? Will the new addition cut down the food preparation time? Enable you to cook ahead more easily? Make kitchen chores simpler for children to perform? Convenience features such as automatic timers that enable you to be in other parts of the house while dinner is cooking may be well worth the extra coast, but scrutinize them carefully.

Other things to look for are the UL (Underwriters Laboratory) listing mark, which indicates that the appliance has met certain safety standards, and for major appliances, the AHAM seal (Association of Home Appliance Manufacturers), which indicates that the size and energy efficiency figures given are accurate. Consider other features, such as holders that enable small appliances to be hung on the wall and save the trouble of rummaging in drawers and cabinets. And consider the availability of maintenance for broken machines; if service is not provided on weekends or other times when someone is at home, it may be wise to choose another brand.

Here is a brief guide to kitchen appliances—small and large—that will save time for most people. Only you know whether they will save time for you.

Freezers: A refrigerator with a large freezing compartment—or a separate freezer in addition to your refrigerator—gives you two advantages. The first is that you can store more and therefore shop less; the second is that you can preserve extra portions of the food you cook. Making double quantities of food—enough stew for two dinners, two pound cakes instead of one—takes little additional time and gives you great flexibility. Be sure to date your freezer packages and try to eat them in order of how long they've been frozen.

Chest freezers are less expensive to buy and operate than upright freezers, but they take up more floor space and have to be manually defrosted. Uprights are available in no-frost and manual-defrost models, and the food is easier to reach. New features include polyurethane foam insulation, power-saver switches, nonelectric anticondensation door strips, a signal that warns when freezer power is off, interior lights, removable slide-out storage baskets, and warranties that cover payment for food spoilage if caused by manufacturing defects. Don't rule out a freezer just because you have limited space. There are several compacts as small as five cubic feet.

Note: A refrigerator-freezer with an automatic ice maker is a great time-saver.

Dishwashers: These are still the ultimate time-saving appliances, especially for large families. Today's dishwashers are more efficient than ever—only the crustiest pots need to be prerinsed. Look for a model with a "rinse and hold" cycle that will rinse food from small loads and leave dishes to be washed when the machine is full, saving both water and electricity. Some dishwashers have an extra-powerful pot-washing cycle for heavily soiled dishes; most have a gentle cycle for fine china. There are both portable and built-in models. If you choose a portable, pick one with a work-surface top (many of these are wood chopping blocks) and a faucet coupler that will let you draw water even when the dishwasher is connected to the faucet and in use.

Pressure Cookers: Pressure cookers, which can make stews and tenderize the toughest cuts of meat in minutes, are making a come-back. They're now made in a wide range of sizes, some as small as 2½ quarts, and prepare food in a half to a third of the time of conventional methods.

Microwave Ovens: The new wave in ovens is the microwave, and it may be the working woman's best friend. A microwave oven can cook most foods in a quarter of the time of a conventional oven and can defrost them equally quickly. Some snacks can be heated in a minute or less, and the ovens are particularly good for reheating foods if your family eats dinner at different times. There are four basic types: counter-top models, wall ovens, cooking units that include both a microwave and a conventional oven, and combined ovens that work both conventionally and with microwaves. The original ovens cooked at only one speed, but many of the newer ones offer a range of speeds for greater flexibility. You can cook on paper plates, some plastics, and heat-resistant glass (metal pans should not be used), as well as the wide variety of baking and roasting pans now made especially for mivrowave ovens. Since the interior of the oven doesn't get hot (the microwaves act directly on the food), splatters don't burn on and the surface can easily be cleaned with a damp cloth. Some models have timers and memory devices so that you can instruct the machine to first defrost a roast at one speed, then cook it at another. Some have turntables that rotate the food as it cooks. Other special features include browning pans or browning elements to sear meats, temperature probes for precise cooking (you insert the probe into the food, select a finished cooking temperature, and the oven will cook the food until the temperature is reached, then shut itself off), and ovens that will cook different foods to the right degree of doneness at the same time. Since special features usually add to the cost and the ovens are expensive, think carefully before you buy.

MAKE FRIENDS WITH YOUR MICROWAVE. The first step toward making friends with that new microwave oven in your kitchen is to appreciate it for what it does well and skip the rest. Stop thinking of it as an "oven" doing oven-type things. It isn't a hot, dry cubicle, so don't expect any crisping or browning to take place.

Start to think of your microwave as an appliance that can make your life easier by taking over certain jobs for which it is well suited. Used in combination with your conventional oven and stovetop, the microwave can speed up meal preparation and reduce clean-up time.

Here are some tips:

• A microwave oven does a marvelous job of reheating. Arrange food directly on the dinner plate, heat, and serve. You'll be amazed at the number of pots and pans this eliminates.

For best results, all food should be at the same temperature so it will heat evenly. Place the thickest portion of the meat toward the outside of the plate and cover loosely with plastic wrap. Select a low power setting—50 percent if the food has been refrigerated, 70 percent if it's at room temperature. You can tell the food is ready to eat when moisture beads begin to appear on the plastic wrap and the bottom of the plate feels warm.

Casseroles can be reheated in individual portions or right in the baking dish. The only hitch is that fat often separates out or rises to the surface of a casserole, and fat attracts microwave energy—so stir thoroughly to insure even cooking. Heat for two minutes, rotate the dish, and stir again. Continue cooking until warm.

Breads and pastries are somewhat tricky to warm up. Wrap them in a paper towel to absorb excess moisture and heat until just warm to the touch. Resist the urge to continue until they feel hot—they'll come out hard as golf balls. Four dinner rolls take 18 to 20 seconds. Add four seconds for each additional roll.

• Think combination. Get accustomed to using your microwave oven as you would another appliance—to prepare part of a recipe or meal. Ask yourself, "Which steps could I do faster and easier in the microwave?"

For example, brown pork chops in a ceramic frying pan on the top of the stove. Then pop them into the microwave to finish, linking the browning ability of your conventional stovetop with the speed of the microwave.

• The most common mistake made by novice microwavers is overcooking. Food cooked in a microwave oven doesn't crisp or brown the way you're used to, which leads to the temptation to cook food a little bit more. Don't do it.

Microwaved food continues to cook internally for three to five minutes after it is removed from the oven—or after the oven is turned off. This is called "carryover cooking" or standing time, and it's every bit as important as the actual cooking time. Some recipes specify how much standing time to allow; some don't mention it at all. A good rule of thumb is to wait two minutes for a single portion, three minutes for a double portion, and five minutes for four or more portions.

Other factors that affect cooking time have to do with size, shape, and amount. The larger the food item, the longer it will take to cook. Allow more time for things that are thicker and wider. Microwaves penetrate food only one and a half inches. Hence, the doughnut-shape rule: Food arranged in an open circle cooks more efficiently than in any other pattern or shape.

It's also important to keep in mind that the amount of food in the oven changes the length of the cooking time. No matter what power level you use, there is only a set amount of microwave energy present in the oven. Food completely absorbs this energy. The more food in the oven, the more the energy that must be shared. So, larger amounts of food take longer to cook. If you decide to put in one more item, remember to adjust the time accordingly.

Density is something else to consider. It takes microwaves longer to penetrate food that is compact. Porous foods cook more quickly. That's why you can cook a two-and-a-half-pound meatloaf in much less time than a roast beef of exactly the same weight.

• New microwave accessories appear on the market every time you turn around, and their manufacturers make some extravagant promises. Before you buy anything, live with your microwave for a while to be sure that new gadget will really help you.

Double-check your cupboards for old glass and ceramic utensils you may have long ago banished to oblivion. You use them as is or improvise with them. A nine-inch glass pie plate is the ideal size and shape for many microwaving chores; a large glass bowl with a drinking glass set inside can become a ring mold. Ceramic custard cups can be used for muffins or cupcakes. There's no need to purchase an expensive steamer when a double sheet of plastic wrap performs just as well. An inverted saucer makes an acceptable meat rack, and bacon cooks nicely on a paper plate.

• Improve the appearance of microwaved food with a few tricks of the trade. Roast chicken or turkey needs to be browned and crisped to look its best. You can accomplish this by taking it out of the microwave before it's completely cooked, and place it in a conventional oven set at 425° F; in 10 minutes the bird will be handsomely browned. Dishes with a cream-style sauce, such as macaroni and cheese or potatoes au gratin, can be slipped under the broiler of a conventional oven to brown.

Bread crumbs, toasted and buttered, make an attractive topping for microwaved casseroles. Bacon bits, crumbled fried onions from a can, or toasted almonds add to the appeal of vegetables and fish.

Chocolate, spice, and upside-down cakes come out looking fine. Others need some help. Yellow cake and coffee cake will appear healthier if you dust the greased pan with crushed cookie or graham cracker crumbs. Pie crust brushed with an egg yolk takes on a rich-pastry hue, or brush the baked shell with boiled, strained apricot jam to give the crust a golden glow.

• The manufacturer's cookbook is your reliable partner and bible. Besides recipes, it contains a wealth of information—charts and more charts for microwaving both fresh and frozen vegetables, fruits, meats, and all sorts of convenience foods.

The opening chapters of the cookbook usually explain how micro-waving works, in terms that nonengineers can understand. Take it to bed with you some night instead of your usual mystery. Not as exciting perhaps, but guaranteed to put you to sleep just the same.

Slow Cookers: At the other end of the spectrum, slow cookers enable you to cook a good meal while you are at work. Many companies offer models with removable crocks. You can prepare and refrigerate the dish the night before, insert the crock in the cooker, plug it in the next morning, and refrigerate the leftovers that night—all in the same con-tainer. Removable crocks can also go into the dishwasher for easier cleaning. Some brands offer a choice of cooking settings and will even shift automatically from high to low.

Toaster-Ovens: These don't cook most foods faster than conven-tional ovens, but they don't have to be preheated, which saves time. They're also easy to use, which makes them perfect for children, especially at lunch and snack time. All will bake, make toast, or top-brown foods. Like microwave ovens, they use less energy than regular electric ovens and don't heat the house up in hot weather. Toaster-ovens come in a variety of sizes; some include a standard pop-up toaster for bread. Certain models also allow you to broil foods, but many do not, so check carefully before buying.

Pressure Fryers: This new kind of fryer-pressure cooker can produce crispy fried chicken in 15 minutes. All you do is put the cooker on the range, heat oil in it, brown the chicken or other food, close the special lock top, and in minutes your dinner is ready.

Mini Deep-Fat Fryers: These relatively new electric devices both heat the oil for frying and store it later on. What you save is the time involved in pouring oil into a pot or frying pan, then straining it into a jar and cleaning the pot or pan afterwards. The oil can be used several times before it needs to be discarded and the fryer scrubbed out.

Bag Sealers: These products offer another option in freezing foods and saving leftovers. The food is put in special boilable bags and tightly sealed by the heating strip inside the appliance. The food can be refrigerated or frozen right in the bag and reheated by placing the bag in a pan of boiling water. Food reheated in this way keeps its original freshness and produces no dirty pots, and the cooking time is much less than that of a meal frozen whole in a casserole dish. All brands have a selection of bag sizes from family-meal size to individual portions. Some offer a continuous roll so you can custom-cut the size bag you need. Also made are models that will seal different foods in separate sections of the same bag and machines that seal regular plastic bags in addition to the boilable kind.

Mixers: Beating dough and batter and whipped cream by machine is always faster than doing it by hand. There are two types of mixers: Portable mixers take up less room, cost less money, and have to be held while you use them. Standard models sit on the counter and will mix the batter while you do something else. Some portables now have stands, and some mixer heads of standard versions may be removed and used as portables. The newest feature on several standard mixers is a dough hook for breadmaking, but many lines offer a wide variety of attachments.

Blenders: To mince, chop, puree, or grate foods, the blender is still the standard appliance and a lot faster than chopping food by hand or using a mortar and pestle or a food mill. Blenders can reconstitute frozen orange juice, make frothy milk shakes or cocktails, or grate enough cheese for a dish of Welsh rarebit all in seconds. Some models even cook as they blend. Look for one with a removable center cap that allows you to add ingredients while the machine is running, a dishwasher-safe container (some have jars in which you can both blend and store foods), and a cutting mechanism that is easy to remove and clean.

Food Processors: Combining many of the functions of a blender and a mixer with those of a meat grinder, a slicer, and a whole range of other tools, the food processor is the most popular new appliance to come out in years. It's also a great deal more expensive than most other appliances (though competition has produced some lower-cost models), so consider your needs and the tools you already own before buying. Though processors are best known for whizzing through the numerous procedures required for elaborate recipes, they are just as useful for more mundane tasks. The food is pushed through a chute with a special plunger and falls into a bowl under the cutting disk. Most units have three disks—a chopper-grinder, a slicer, and a shredder. Others add a plastic blade for light mixing jobs, a ripple cutter, juilienne disk, French-fry cutter, or thick-slicing disk. You can make a week's worth of salad to keep in the crisper, chop onions, grind your own extra-lean hamburger, and prepare the vegetables for a stew almost instantly. The components of a food processor can be easily taken apart for cleaning, and most are dishwasher-safe. Because there are so many brands and features to consider, it's worth attending a food-processor demonstration, checking with friends, and asking to see the use-care booklets. Other useful features to look for: a handle on the bowl to make it easier to hold; food pushers that double as measuring cups; and food chutes that are tall and wide enough to process as much food as possible. One company now makes a food-processor unit that also comes with a separate blender attachment. Food processors are often discounted, so shop around.

Appendix II
SUPERMARKET STRATEGY

Convenience foods may have cut down on cooking time, but shopping for them takes longer than ever. In fact, women spend the equivalent of one full working day a week on shopping and shopping-related travel. Fifty years ago they spent less than two hours on these activities. However, a reverse trend may be in the offing—especially when it comes to food shopping—and working wives are leading the way. Those of us with jobs outside the home often market less than full-time housewives; over half make a major foray into food stores only once a week or less. But even the most efficient among us sometimes find ourselves running back during the week to pick up another carton of milk or loaf of bread, and the time spent in transit and at the checkout counter rapidly mounts up.

It takes planning to avoid wasting precious after-work time in mini expeditions to the market. Post a large pad or blackboard in the kitchen and require each member of the family to note on it when his favorite food is running low. Get in the habit of sketching out menus for the entire week so you'll be sure to have the necessary ingredients on hand. And since no one can predict household consumption down to the last mouthful, add extra snack items, juvenile staples, and meal stretchers to your list, plus a few company frills—a fancy frozen dessert, perhaps, and a crock of cheese.

You might want to plan your menus with an eye toward using up the most perishable produce first. But don't feel that you have to buy everything "fresh"—and therefore very frequently—in order to feed your family well. Frozen vegetables often have a higher vitamin content than their unprocessed counterparts because the large growers station their processing machines right in the fields and scoop up the vegetables the moment they hit their peak. Canned and packaged products are often highly nutritious, too, of course, and they offer the further advantage of long life in your pantry. Since these prepared foods are indispensable to a once-a-week marketing regimen, you'll want to stock them routinely.

Thinking may be the first step in getting ready to market, but you also have to go on to see what's in your larder and often *feel* it as well. (Many a respectable-looking cereal box turns out to be totally empty when shaken.) And you'll want to check your other cabinets and closets for toothpaste, cleaning supplies, and the like. When you've completed this tour of inspection, transfer all your jottings from the running list to the final marketing list. Finally, flip through your coupons and clip to your list the ones you want to use.

Now that you're ready to shop, where should you go? It's best to find one convenient, well-stocked supermarket and stick with it. You will probably save as much money in the long run by buying its specials as you would by hunting for bargains all over town—and you will certainly save time and effort. Statistically, as a working mother you probably do confine yourself to one market, but a Dallas area survey indicates that the younger you are the less likely you are to shop around, whether you're working or not.

Once you get to know a market well, you can zip down its aisles plucking goods from their familiar resting places almost by rote. If you arrange your shopping list by category and aisle, you'll save even more time. Crossing off each item as you put it into your cart will further speed the process by minimizing the chances of overlooking something that might require you to double back or, even worse, make a return trip. When you reach the checkout counter, make one final bid to save time: Ask the packer to put all the frozen foods into one bag, all the meats in another, and all the dairy products in a third, to expedite unpacking when you get home.

In some instances you will have to develop special strategies to enable you to market just once a week. If you don't use a car when you shop, for example, you will want to look around for a supermarket that will deliver. Often the charge for this service is nominal, but even where it isn't, it has to be cheap compared to the value of the time you'd spend making repeated trips to the market. You might also want to find out where you can order groceries by phone—when you're really in a rush, this option can be a lifesaver. Other ways to save time include subscribing to a freezer plan, having dairy products delivered, and ordering cleaning supplies and paper goods from a restaurant-supply house.

The greatest time-saver of all, of course, is having someone else shop for you and, according to the Bureau of Advertising, 13 percent of all working wives do just that. Surveys show that husbands help out with shopping far more than with other household chores. To insure good results, you may want to give your husband an extremely specific list in the beginning, with the quantity and brand name noted next to each item. Older children also enjoy marketing—at least compared to cleaning up their rooms—and they can become quite proficient at it if you teach them how to read labels and reject dented cans.

As the week goes by, the supply of food will run low—no matter who obtains it—and you will be tempted to pick up a few things on the way home from work. Don't. Remind yourself how much more time you have by marketing just once a week and how much more money you have because you're not squandering it on impulse purchases.

Appendix III
COOKING FOR
SURPRISE GUESTS

When people you care about drop by unexpectedly or call to say that they're in town, including them in your dinner plans doesn't have to be a production. No special planning is necessary. Real friends visit because they enjoy being with you and your family and because they feel comfortable in your home. They're not looking for anything fancy—they'll expect and enjoy potluck.

Your whole family probably will appreciate an easygoing approach to company, too. Your husband and kids will like feeling free to bring friends and co-workers home on short notice.

But to do this sort of thing, there are some necessities you will want to keep in reserve. With them in your cupboard, you'll be able to stretch or improvise what you have on hand. The following is a list of food supplies to store on an "emergency shelf" in your cupboard, refrigerator, and freezer:

Emergency Shelf

Canned beef broth
Canned chicken broth
Canned stewed tomatoes
Prepared spaghetti sauce
Canned marinated garbanzos, three-bean salad, artichoke hearts, or
   pickled beets
Biscuit mix
Canned fruit
Prepared salad dressings
Assorted pasta
Rice
French bread, unsliced white or whole wheat loaves, or dinner rolls
   (in freezer)

Canned mushroom soup
Canned cream of celery soup
Canned tuna
Canned salmon

Appendix IV
BASIC COOKING
TERMINOLOGY

Bake: To cook by dry heat, usually in the oven. When applied to meats and vegetables, this is called roasting.

Barbecue: To roast meats very slowly on a spit or rack over heat, basting with a seasoned sauce.

Baste: To moisten foods while cooking with meat drippings, melted fat, or sauces, to prevent drying and to add flavor.

Blanch: To remove skins from fruits, vegetables, or nuts by letting them stand in boiling water until skins peel off easily.

Blend: To mix thoroughly two or more ingredients.

Boil: Bring to boiling or *bring to a boil* signifies the step before cooking. You'll know that water or any liquid is reaching that point when bubbles appear at the bottom, rise to the top, and then break. When all liquid is in motion, it has come to a boil. Boil means to cook at the boiling point. When this point is reached, adjust heat to maintain it. *Boil rapidly* means the point at which liquid goes into rapid motion; the surface breaks into small lumpy waves. *Full, rolling boil* means the point at which the liquid rises in the pan, then tumbles into waves that can't be stirred down.

Braise: To brown meat or vegetables in a small amount of hot fat and cook slowly, tightly covered. In some recipes you add other liquids after the initial browning.

Broil: To cook directly under a flame or heating unit or over an open fire or grill.

Chop: To cut food into smaller pieces, usually with a large knife and a cutting board. One hand holds knife tip on the board, the other moves the blade up and down, cutting through the food.

Cream: To beat shortening with a wooden spoon or beater until smooth, creamy, and light. Usually applied to shortening when combined with sugar; for example, in making cakes.

Cube: To cut a solid into little cubes about ½ inch to 1 inch in size.

Dice: To cube, but smaller—less than ½ inch in size.

Dredge: To coat with a powdered substance, such as flour.

Flambé: To cover a food with brandy or cognac, and so forth; then light and serve flaming.

Fold: To combine two ingredients—more often than not, beaten egg whites and batter—very gently with a wire whisk or rubber scraper, using an under-and-over motion, until thoroughly mixed.

Fricassee: To braise fowl, veal, or other meat, cut into pieces, in a small amount of liquid.

Glacé: To coat with a thin sugar syrup cooked to the crack stage.

Glaze: To cover with aspic; to coat with a thin sugar syrup; to cover with melted fruit jelly.

Grate: To tear off coarse-to-fine particles of food with a hand grater or mechanical device.

Julienne: To cut potatoes or vegetables into matchlike sticks.

Knead: To work and press dough hard with the heels of your hands, so the dough becomes stretched and elastic. Usually done to bread and other yeast doughs.

Marinate: To soak food, mainly meat, in acid such as lemon juice or tomato juice, or in an oil-acid mixture such as French dressing.

Pan-Broil: To cook, uncovered, on a hot surface, usually a skillet. The fat is poured off as it accumulates.

Pan-Fry: To cook or fry on top of range in a hot, uncovered skillet with little or no fat.

Parboil: To cook food in a boiling liquid until partially done.

Pare: To cut away coverings of vegetables and fruits.

Peel: To strip or slip off outer coverings of some vegetables or fruits.

Plank: To bake or boil meat, fish, or vegetables on a wooden or metal plank.

Poach: To cook eggs, fish, or vegetables in liquid at or below simmering.

Pot-Roast: To brown meat in a small amount of fat, then finish cooking in a small amount of liquid.

Puree: To work fruits or vegetables through a sieve or food mill or blend in an electric blender until food is pulpy.

Sauté: To fry foods golden and tender in a small amount of fat on top of the range.

Scald: To heat liquids like milk almost to boiling; tiny bubbles will appear at edge.

Score: To cut narrow gashes partway through fat in meats before cooking.

Sear: To brown surface of meat over high heat, either on top of range or in oven.

Shred: To cut or tear in long, narrow pieces.

Simmer: To cook just below boiling point; heat is adjusted to maintain this stage.

Skewer: To thread foods, such as meat, fish, poultry, and vegetables, on a wooden or metal skewer so they hold their shape during cooking.

Sliver: To cut or split into long, thin strips, with a knife on a cutting board.

Steam: To cook by steam in a closed container.

Steep: To let a food stand in hot liquid below boiling, to extract flavor, color, or both.

Stew: To cook foods very slowly—always below the boiling point—in enough liquid to cover.

Whip: To rapidly beat eggs, heavy cream, et cetera, in order to incorporate air and expand volume.

Appendix V
HOW TO MEASURE CORRECTLY

1. Use only standard measuring cups and spoons. Any recipe you follow has been tested with standard equipment.

2. Make all measurements level.

3. In measuring dry ingredients or fats, use the standardized metal cups that come in nests and hold ¼, ⅓, ½, and 1 cup.

4. In measuring dry ingredients, heap the cup or spoon to overflowing; then level off excess with a straight-edge knife or spatula.

5. In measuring fats, bring to room temperature if stored in refrigerator, then press firmly into spoon or cup and level off with straight-edge knife or spatula. One stick of butter or margarine measures ½ cup or 8 tablespoons.

6. When measuring liquids, use the standard glass liquid measuring cup, with lip, marked off in quarters and thirds. Always place cup on a flat surface and measure at eye level.

7. When recipe calls for sifted flour, sift before you measure. Never pack the flour down by banging the cup on the table.

8. Brown sugar should always be packed firmly into the measuring cup or spoon, then leveled off with a knife or spatula. If lumpy, roll with rolling pin before measuring.

9. When measuring molasses, syrup, or honey, pour liquid into a cup or spoon. Do not dip measuring utensil into the heavy liquid. Scrape out thoroughly with a rubber scraper, all liquid that clings to inside.

10. If confectioner's sugar looks lumpy, it is advisable to roll it with a rolling pin before measuring. If recipe calls for sifted confectioner's sugar, press through sieve to sift.

Common Food Weights and Measures

Dash	Less than $\frac{1}{8}$ tsp
1 tablespoon	3 teaspoons
4 tablespoons	$\frac{1}{4}$ cup
$5\frac{1}{3}$ tablespoons	$\frac{1}{3}$ cup
8 tablespoons	$\frac{1}{2}$ cup
12 tablespoons	$\frac{3}{4}$ cup
16 tablespoons	1 cup
1 fluid ounce	2 tablespoons
1 cup	$\frac{1}{2}$ pint (liquid)
2 cups	1 pint
2 pints (4 cups)	1 quart
4 quarts	1 gallon
8 quarts	1 peck (dry)
4 pecks	1 bushel
16 ounces	1 pound

Appendix VI
FREEZING CHART

Appropriate Maximum Storage Life of Some Common Prepared and Precooked Foods

Biscuits, baked	2 months
Cakes, fruit	12 months
Cakes, nonfat angel, baked	4 months
sponge, baked	4 months
Cakes with shortening, baked	4 to 9 months
Casserole dishes, prepared	1 to 4 months
Cookies, baked or unbaked	12 months
Ice cream, commercial*	2 to 3 weeks
homemade	1 month
Muffins, baked	2 months
Pies, fruit, baked or unbaked	3 to 4 months
Pie shells, baked or unbaked	$1\frac{1}{2}$ to 2 months
Sandwiches	1 to 2 months
Soups	6 months
Yeast rolls, baked	12 months
half-baked	12 months

*Half-gallon or gallon containers may be economical if ice cream is stored properly and used within 2 or 3 weeks. Each time ice cream is removed, put moisture vapor-proof paper directly on remainder to keep ice crystals from forming. Never refreeze defrosted ice-cream—harmful bacteria may have developed.

Appendix VII
USEFUL FOOD TERMS

A la king: Food, such as fowl and bland meats, served in a rich cream or white sauce.

Aspic: Meat or vegetable jelly, sometimes with gelatine added, used as a garnish or to mold meats, fish, fowl, or vegetables.

Au gratin: Food mixed with cream or white sauce, covered with bread crumbs or grated cheese, and baked or broiled until the surface is browned.

Au jus: Meat served in its natural juices.

Au lait: Beverage made and served with milk. Coffee, for example.

Au naturel: Food plainly cooked or served in its natural state.

Bar-le-duc: Fruit preserve made from white or red currants.

Batter: Any mixture of dry ingredients and liquid that is stirred or beaten and can be poured or dropped from a spoon.

Bavarian: A dessert pudding made with a gelatine and cream base.

Béarnaise: Hollandaise sauce with shallots, tarragon, chervil, and other seasonings added.

Béchamel: Cream sauce made with chicken and veal stock.

Bisque: (1) A rich cream soup, usually made from fish or shellfish. (2) A rich frozen dessert made from cream, macaroons, and nuts.

Blanquette: A meat or vegetable stew made with a cream or white sauce.

Bombe: A melon or round mold lined with one kind of ice cream and filled with another kind of ice cream or sherbet.

Bordelaise: Brown sauce made with beef stock or bouillon and wine.

Bouillabaisse: Hearty French soup made with large pieces of fish and shellfish.

Brochette: Small spit or skewer used for broiling meat cubes.

Canapé: An appetizer of highly seasoned food, usually served on little pieces of crisp toast or crackers.

Caviar: Prepared, salted roe (or eggs) of sturgeon and other large fish. Usually served as an appetizer.

Charlotte: A molded dessert, usually made with gelatine and flavored whipped cream, with cake or lady fingers outlining the mold.

Chaud-froid: Literally "hot-cold." Gelatine sauce made with white-sauce base, used to coat cold meat, poultry, and fish.

Chiffonade: A mixture of finely chopped fresh herbs, used to season soups and salads.

Chowder: A soup or stew made with fish, shellfish—such as clams or lobster—and/or vegetables.

Cobbler: A deep-dish fruit pie made with a top covering of rich pastry or biscuit dough.

Compote: A variety of stewed fruit served cold in a syrup.

Condiment: A seasoning, such as salt, pepper, spices, herbs. Relishes are also spoken of as condiments.

Conserve: Fruit preserve made with more than one fruit, often with nuts and raisins added.

Court bouillon: A richly flavored stock made from fish.

Crepe: A thin, rich pancake, served with filling and sauce as a main dish or dessert.

Croquettes: Finely chopped or ground meat, fish, fowl, et cetera, mixed with thick cream sauce, shaped into patties or cones, dipped into egg and cracker crumbs and fried until crisp on the outside.

Croutons: Fried or toasted cubes of bread. Used frequently in soups and salads.

Demitasse: Small cups of strong coffee, served after dinner.

Dough: A mixture of dry ingredients, such as flour, and liquid that is stiff enough to handle or knead. Bread and biscuit dough are examples.

Eclair: A small, finger-shape pastry filled with custard or whipped cream.

Entree: (1) The main dish of an American family meal. (2) At a formal dinner, a small serving of food, usually fish, served before the main course.

Filet mignon: Tender, cross-cut slice of beef from the tenderloin.

Fondant: A type of candy made from sugar syrup that is kneaded to creaminess.

Fondue: A cheese luncheon or supper dish.

Fritters: Mixture of vegetables, fruit or meat, and batter, fried crisp in hot fat.

Goulash: A thick meat stew flavored with vegetables and paprika. Usually associated with Hungarian cookery.

Grenadine: Syrup used for sweetening mixed drinks; made from pomegranate juice.

Gumbo: A richly flavored soup thickened with okra.

Hollandaise: A sauce made with eggs, butter, and lemon juice or vinegar. Served hot or cold with vegetables or fish.

Hors d'oeuvre: Appetizer course; usually small pieces of finger food.

Ice: A frozen dessert made from fruit juices, sugar, and water. Sometimes gelatine or egg whites are added.

Kirsch: Cherry liqueur, mainly produced in Switzerland.

Kisses: Tiny dessert meringues.

Légumes: Vegetable seeds (peas, beans, lentils), usually referred to as such in the dried state.

Macaroons: Small cakes made from egg whites, sugar, and ground almonds or almond paste.

Macedoine: A combination of different fruits or vegetables.

Marguerite: A salted cracker spread with boiled frosting, sprinkled with nuts, coconut, or chocolate pieces, and baked until golden.

Marinade: An acid (tomato or lemon juice) or a mixture of oil and acid (French dressing) in which food is soaked to develop flavor and tenderness.

Marrons: Chestnuts; usually preserved or glacéed.

Marzipan: A candylike paste made with finely ground almonds and sugar.

Minestrone: A thick Italian soup made with vegetables and pasta.

Mocha: A coffee or coffee-chocolate combination of flavors, used in desserts and beverages.

Mousse: (1) A dessert of sweetened, frozen whipped cream with fruit and nuts. (2) A vegetable or meat dish thickened with gelatine and served as a main dish.

Parfait: A dessert of ice cream, fruit, and whipped cream, or a frozen mixture of egg whites or yolks cooked with hot syrup and combined with whipped cream.

Pâté de foie gras: A smooth, richly seasoned paste made from goose livers.

Patty shell: A shell made from puff paste or pastry and filled with creamed shellfish, chicken, and the like.

Petits fours: Very small, iced-all-over cakes. Served at tea parties or as a dessert accompaniment for ice cream or fruit.

Pilaf: A main dish made with meat, fish, or fowl and rice, vegetables, and spices.

Rabbit or rarebit: A mixture of cheese, eggs, seasonings, and white sauce, usually served over toast.

Ragout: A thick, well-seasoned French stew made with meats, vegetables, and herbs.

Ramekins: Small, individual casserole dishes.

Ravioli: Large noodles filled with finely minced meat, vegetables, or cheese, then cooked in boiling stock or water.

Relish: A highly seasoned food accompaniment, like chutney, India relish, or olives. Used to enhance the flavor of other foods.

Rissole: A nicely seasoned meat mixture, wrapped in rich pastry and fried in deep fat.

Roux: A cooked mixture of butter and flour, used to thicken soups and sauces.

Sherbet: A frozen mixture of fruit juice, sugar, egg whites, water or milk. Served as dessert or as a main-dish accompaniment.

Smorgasbord: Swedish appetizer or entree course consisting of a large variety of foods, usually set up as a buffet.

Soufflé: A puffy, airy, hot dish made light with egg whites mixed gently with white sauce. Usually cheese, fish, meat, et cetera, are added. Also a dessert, most frequently made with chocolate or fruit.

Stock: The richly flavored liquid in which meat, fish, fowl, or vegetables have been cooked. Used in sauces, soups, and general cookery.

Timbale: A baked, unsweetened custard in which finely chopped meats, fish, fowl, or vegetables have been mixed.

Torte: Very rich layers of cake made with crumbs, eggs, and nuts, topped with whipped cream and fruit.

Truffles: Fungus that grows underground; used for garnishing and flavoring.

Tutti-frutti: A mixture of many kinds of fruit.

Velouté: Rich white sauce made with ham, chicken, or veal stock, seasoned with bouquet garni.

Vinaigrette: Sauce made of oil, vinegar, and seasonings.

Vol-au-vent: Patties of puff paste, to be filled with meat, fish, or poultry.

White sauce: A combination of butter, flour, milk, cream, or stock, seasoned and cooked until smooth and creamy.

Appendix VIII
GUIDE FOR USING
HERBS AND SPICES

Allspice: Mincemeat and pumpkin pies, plum pudding, cookies, cakes, and some vegetables.

Anise: Cookies, candies, sweet pickles, beverage flavoring, coffee cakes, and sweet rolls.

Basil: Tomato dishes, soups, stews, beans, peas, and squash. Often sprinkled on lamb before cooking.

Bay leaves: Pickling spice mixtures, soups, stews, fish chowder, tomato and seafood aspics, and variety meats.

Caraway: Rye bread, rolls, cakes, cheeses, cottage cheese, sauerkraut, and coleslaw. Add to turnips and asparagus when cooking.

Cardamom: Danish pastry, coffee cakes, custards, cookies, and fruits.

Celery seed: Pickling spice mixtures, sauces, salads, salad dressings, fish, and vegetables.

Chili powder: Seafood-cocktail sauces, barbecue sauces, meatloaf, hamburger, and stews.

Chives: Salads, salad dressings, scrambled eggs, omelets, cream cheese, cottage cheese, and butter.

Cinnamon: Baked apples, puddings, and hot cereals. Combine with sugar for cinnamon toast.

Cloves: Whole: roast pork, ham, pickled fruits, spicy syrups, and meat gravies. Ground: baked goods, chocolate pudding, stews, and vegetables.

Curry powder: Sauces for eggs, vegetables, fish, and meat. Also in French dressing, scalloped tomatoes, clam and fish chowders, and pea soup.

Dill seed: Pickles, rye, and pumpernickel bread, soups, salads, sauces, meat and fish dishes, potatoes, and coleslaw.

Dry mustard: Pickles, cabbage, sauerkraut, coleslaw, relishes, potato salad, cream soups, cheese, egg, and seafood dishes.

Garlic: Soups, salads, sauces, meats, fish, and casserole dishes.

Ginger: Cookies, spice cakes, gingerbread, pot roasts, stews, chicken, soups, and fish dishes.

Mace: Pound cakes, fish and meat stuffings, peach and cherry pies, fruit cakes, cobblers, oyster stew, creamed eggs, and whipped cream.

Marjoram: Vegetables, lamb, mutton, sausage, stews, and poultry stuffings.

Mint: Drinks, fruit cups, jellies, salads, fish sauces, vegetables, and meat sauces (lamb).

Nutmeg: Baked goods, puddings, vegetables, beverages, soups, and beef and fish dishes.

Oregano: Tomato dishes, vegetables, and salads.

Paprika: Used as a garnish for colorless foods.

Parsley: Cheese, eggs, fish, meats, poultry, salads, sauces, and vegetables.

Poppy seed: Topping for cookies, pastries, rolls, bread, noodles, and salad greens.

Rosemary: Boiled potatoes, turnips, and cauliflower. Sprinkle on beef and fish before cooking.

Saffron: Rolls, cakes, and rice.

Sage: Stuffings for pork and poultry.

Savory: Meats, poultry, fish dishes, scrambled eggs, sauerkraut, cabbage, peas, and salads.

Sesame seed: Cookies, rolls, candies, chicken dishes, French bread, green beans, and asparagus.

Tarragon: Chicken dishes and stuffings, green and seafood salads, and lamb chops.

Thyme: Clam chowder, fish sauces, croquettes, fresh tomato salads, and egg dishes.

Appendix IX
MORE KITCHEN TIPS

Here are some additional tips that will make your quick cooking even easier.

Leftover cooked squash or sweet potatoes, drained and mashed, may be used in place of canned pumpkin in any recipe for pie, cake, or cookies. Use the same amount of the substitute vegetable that is specified for pumpkin.

Almonds are much easier to slice or sliver if you plunge them into boiling water for 1 minute before you try to cut them. (If you want to remove the skins, they will slip off easily at this point.) Pat the almonds dry, slice, and spread out on a towel or cookie sheet to dry.

For a quick meatless pasta sauce, chop whatever fresh vegetables you have on hand and simmer in prepared marinara sauce just until tender. This is an especially good idea when you have a large supply of your family's least favorite vegetable.

To substitute all-purpose flour for cake flour: Measure 1 level cup of all-purpose flour; remove 2 tablespoons of flour and replace with 2 tablespoons of cornstarch.

Make your rich chocolate cake taste even richer: Dust the greased baking pan with cocoa instead of flour.

Keep a plastic container in your freezer for storing small amounts of leftover vegetables. Then, when you make soup, add them to the pot. Don't bother to defrost the vegetables—just slip them into the soup during the last 10 minutes of cooking.

To cook bacon without fuss, separate the slices and arrange on a rack in a baking pan. Bake at 400° F for 8–10 minutes. This eliminates having to watch and turn the bacon and cuts down on spattering.

To break up ground beef while browning for spaghetti sauce or chili, use a potato masher instead of a fork. It will do the job in half the time. A potato masher is also handy for crushing whole tomatoes in the sauce.

Egg whites freeze very well—yolks don't. To keep leftover yolks fresh for several days, put them in a cup and cover with water. Seal the top tightly with plastic wrap and refrigerate.

Meatloaf will be less apt to crack if you spoon or brush a little cold water over the top before baking.

An easy way to free the sticky remains of cheese from your grater is to rub a raw potato over the nubs.

To slice a hard-boiled egg without crumbling the yolk, dip the knife or egg slicer in ice-cold water beforehand.

For fluffy pancakes that will practically float from the griddle to the table, replace the milk in the recipe with sparkling water.

You'll get cheers from the children when you serve skinless pudding. To achieve this perfection, spread plastic wrap directly on the creamy surface immediately after pouring the hot dessert into dishes.

When cooking sauerkraut, add an apple, quartered and peeled, to the pot. The fruit mellows the flavor of the dish.

Frozen fish will taste fresher if you thaw it in buttermilk. Place the frozen fish in a glass or ceramic dish and cover with the liquid. The soaking helps to draw out that deep-freeze taste.

Boilovers won't occur if you insert a toothpick between the lid and the pot. This allows steam to escape.

Here's a recipe for iced tea to pass on to the kids: First thing in the morning, fill a 1-quart, clear glass pitcher or jar with cold water and drop in 4 tea bags. Place the container on a sunny windowsill. At dinnertime, just add lemon, sugar, and ice to the delicious "sun" tea.

When adding nuts or dried fruits to cake batter, coat them with some flour to prevent them from sinking to the bottom of the pan during baking.

If your brown sugar has turned into a rock, put it in an overproof dish in a 300° F oven for about 10 minutes to soften.

Piecrust will be more tender if you roll it between two sheets of waxed paper instead of adding extra flour. Use a glass or dark-colored pie plate for a crisper lower crust.

To prevent the bottom piecrust from getting soggy, brush with egg yolk before adding the filling.

It's easier to slice or cut meat if it's partially frozen rather than completely thawed.

A remedy for overdone biscuits (too crispy and crusty) is to cover them with damp paper towels for a few minutes. The biscuits will soften.

A quick, inexpensive copper cleaner: Combine 2 tablespoons of salt with 1 cup of white vinegar. Use a rag to wipe the pot clean with the mixture.

It's easy to unmold gelatin if you lightly oil the pan before filling it.

For a small amount of lemon juice, instead of slicing a whole lemon, cut an X in the skin and squeeze out what you need. The lemon will keep better since the pulp isn't exposed.

To avoid lumps, use granulated flour instead of regular flour to thicken gravies and sauces. If you're using regular flour, put it in a small jar, add some water, cover tightly, and shake. Then add it to the stock or drippings.

You can ripen some fruits (such as avocados, peaches, pears, or plums) extra quickly by placing them in a closed brown-paper bag for a day.

To remove fat from stew or soup, refrigerate it overnight. If you're in a hurry, pop it into the freezer for a while, then lift off the hardened fat.

A poached egg will keep its shape if you stir some vinegar into the water before dropping the egg in.

Coat the inside of the measuring cup with oil before measuring molasses, syrup, or honey. It will pour out easily.

Cut marshmallows with wet scissors; cut dried fruit with heated scissors.

Next time you find your kitchen filled with black smoke because the juices from a baking pie have dripped overboard and are burning away on the oven floor, remember this: Salt poured over the burning mess will bring the smoking to a halt and make the drippings easy to scrape up when the oven cools.

After you've chopped a large onion or a few garlic cloves, squeeze a little lemon juice into your hands and rub well. It will remove the strong smell.

Plastic wrap is sometimes hard to handle because it clings to itself or flies up and sticks to something else. This irritating property is put to rest with a simple tactic: Store plastic wrap in the freezer compartment of your refrigerator. When you remove it to use, it'll be manageable.

To banish the odor of fried fish or some other unpleasant smell, put a piece of orange skin on an electric burner and turn the heat to low. Let the orange skin burn slowly for about 10 minutes; turn off the heat and let the orange peel remain on the burner for a little while longer. It will give off a pungent, spicy smell. If you own a gas stove, you can put an apple stuck with four cloves on a piece of foil in the oven at 350° F. Leave it to bake for 30–40 minutes. Turn off the heat and open the oven door to let the fragrance fill the kitchen.

To poach an egg so that it keeps its shape, place the egg, uncracked, in a saucepan of boiling water and leave it there for 10 seconds. Remove the egg and crack it into a cup or saucer. Slip the egg back into the boiling water and simmer until firm. You will have a beautiful poached egg.

To loosen cake layers that have been allowed to cool in the pans, gently warm the bottoms of the pans over low heat on top of the stove for about 30 seconds. The layers will turn out easily.

If you have small amounts of meat left over after a meal, prepare half sandwiches. Wrap them tightly and freeze.

To hide strong cooking odors, measure 1 tablespoon of rosemary into a small skillet. Heat gently until it begins to smoke, remove from heat, and the rosemary will continue to give off a pleasant natural aroma for quite a while.

Index

smoked pork and sauerkraut, 47
spareribs with sauerkraut, 54
spinach and 3-bean, 48
stuffed roast chicken, 59
Swiss steak, 55

ziti, baked, 106
zucchini:
  boats, 17
  -cheese custard, 91